# WOOD MOSAIC
# PROJECTS

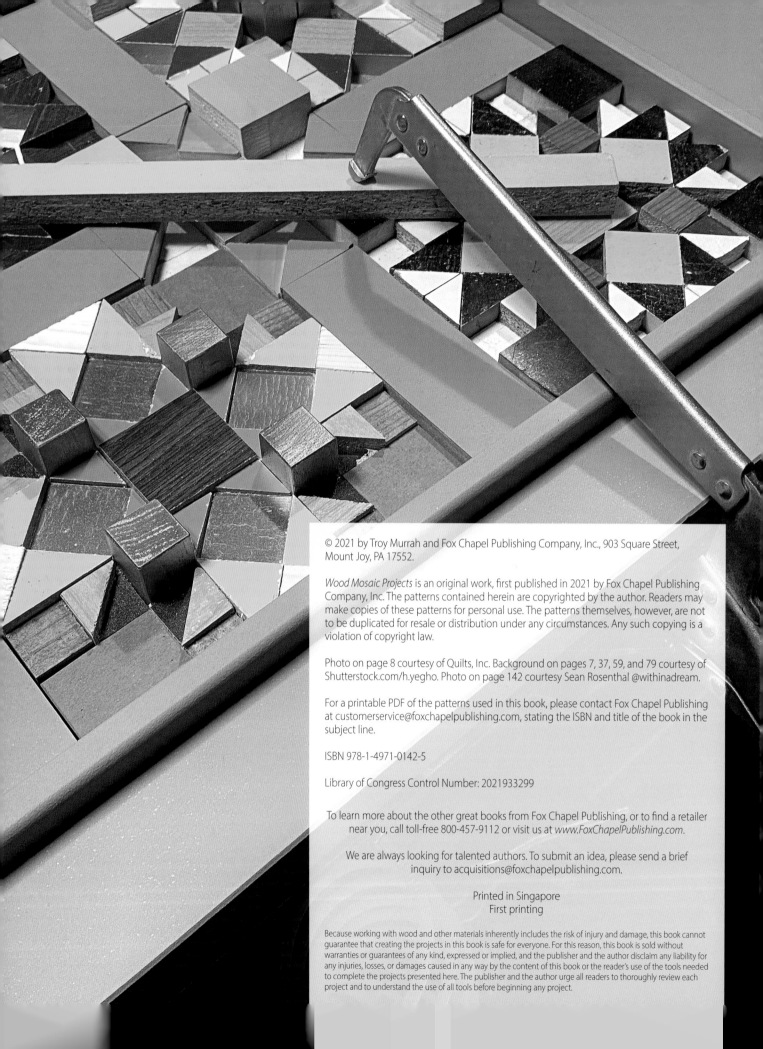

Photo on page 8 courtesy of Quilts, Inc. Background on pages 7, 37, 59, and 79 courtesy of Shutterstock.com/h.yegho. Photo on page 142 courtesy Sean Rosenthal @withinadream.

For a printable PDF of the patterns used in this book, please contact Fox Chapel Publishing at customerservice@foxchapelpublishing.com, stating the ISBN and title of the book in the subject line.

ISBN 978-1-4971-0142-5

Library of Congress Control Number: 2021933299

To learn more about the other great books from Fox Chapel Publishing, or to find a retailer near you, call toll-free 800-457-9112 or visit us at *www.FoxChapelPublishing.com*.

We are always looking for talented authors. To submit an idea, please send a brief inquiry to acquisitions@foxchapelpublishing.com.

Printed in Singapore
First printing

# WOOD MOSAIC PROJECTS

## CLASSIC QUILT BLOCK DESIGNS IN WOOD

Troy Murrah

Fox Chapel
PUBLISHING

# Contents

Introduction . . . . . . . . . . . . . . . . . . . . . . . . . . . . . . . . . . . .6

Gallery . . . . . . . . . . . . . . . . . . . . . . . . . . . . . . . . . . . . . . . . . .8

## PART 1: Getting Started

Materials . . . . . . . . . . . . . . . . . . . . . . . . . . . . . . . . . . . . . .20

Tools . . . . . . . . . . . . . . . . . . . . . . . . . . . . . . . . . . . . . . . . . .22

Techniques, Tips, and Tricks . . . . . . . . . . . . . . . . . . . . . .27

## PART 2: Projects

Lattice Square Wall Hanging . . . . . . . . . . . . . . . . . . . . . .36

Prosperity Block Shadowbox . . . . . . . . . . . . . . . . . . . . . .46

Goose Tracks Woodburned Wall Art . . . . . . . . . . . . . . . .58

Star and Wreath Desk Décor . . . . . . . . . . . . . . . . . . . . .68

Radiant Lone Star Wood Tapestry . . . . . . . . . . . . . . . . . .78

Log Cabin Wall Quilt . . . . . . . . . . . . . . . . . . . . . . . . . . . .90

Festival of Stars Door . . . . . . . . . . . . . . . . . . . . . . . . . .100

Pineapple Ice Queen Coffee Table . . . . . . . . . . . . . . . .114

Patterns . . . . . . . . . . . . . . . . . . . . . . . . . . . . . . . . . . . . .130

About the Artist . . . . . . . . . . . . . . . . . . . . . . . . . . . . . . .142

Index . . . . . . . . . . . . . . . . . . . . . . . . . . . . . . . . . . . . . . .143

**36**

**68**

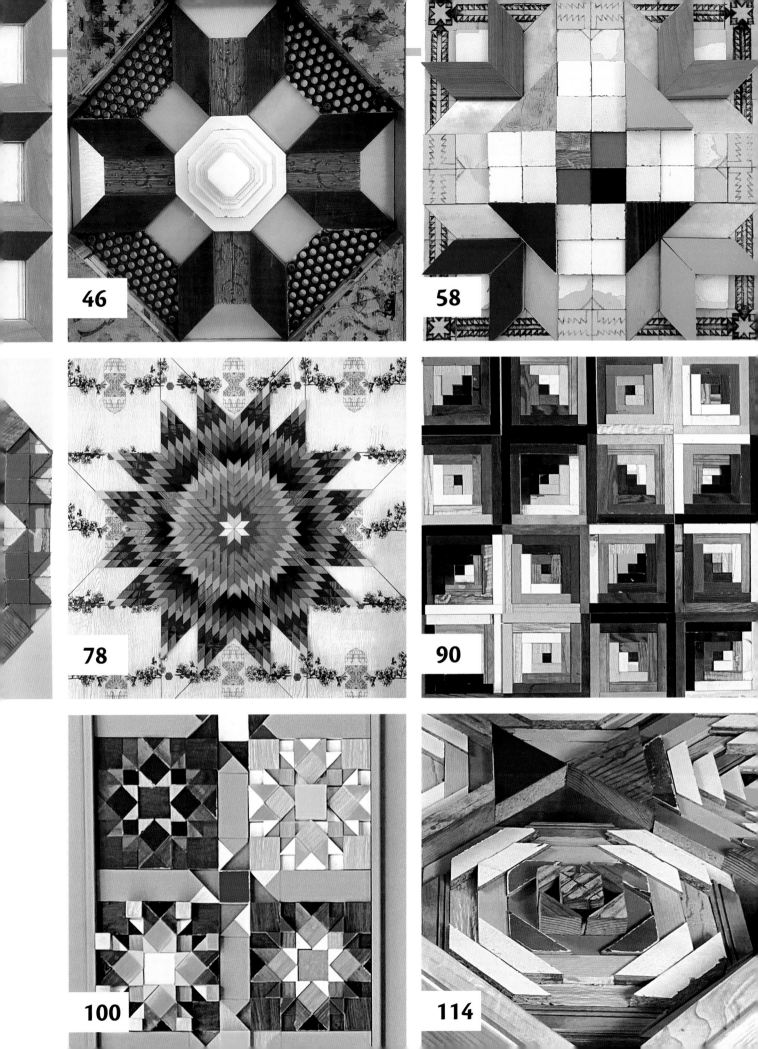

46

58

78

90

100

114

# Introduction

Quilting isn't just for fabric anymore. Combining my inherited family skills of quilting
and carpentry, I taught myself to use thousands of wood fragments, cut from leftover remnants,
to construct elaborate wall hangings that replicate traditional quilt block designs.
Now I'd like to share my technique with you.

This book teaches all the basics you need to know to design and construct your own unique wooden mosaic projects, including how to work with quilt block–inspired patterns, how to cut intricate wood pieces to fit snugly, and tips for adding color and texture to achieve desired effects. It's a gorgeous, creative approach that is meant to inspire you—to motivate you to explore the combined worlds of woodworking and quiltmaking. My aim is to give you a springboard into putting your own unique spin on my original "built quilt" pieces, as I like to call them.

Wood quilts are nothing short of spectacular, and you can follow along with this book's eight achievable projects before branching out to design your own. The projects include small wall art and gift items, medium-sized and more complex pieces, and a stunning coffee table and door that can be completed by even a beginner woodworker. Plus, flip through the gallery to see some of the more advanced pieces I've made that you can use as inspiration for your own designs once you've created a few of the projects.

Importantly, the wood mosaics in this book were not made from freshly-milled lumber sourced from a woodshop—they were made from upcycled scraps collected over time. That's an important part of this book's ethos. For centuries, people have resourcefully used scraps, remnants, and rags to make quilts. Similarly, with these projects, you'll learn to build on your own resourcefulness—to keep an eye open for useful material wherever you go. Anything from leftover floorboards, to discarded shelving, to found material can be cut down and used for these projects. This book will teach you how to turn discarded wood into magic.

I want to uphold tradition and the value of craft while also refreshing the processes and form. These wood mosaic designs link us to historical quilt block compositions while offering a fresh take on them. Your personal inspiration may come from anywhere—your background is likely very different from mine—but we'll explore the practical knowledge needed to create these wood quilts together. I hope to teach you the importance of making things with your hands that can be functional, decorative, and meaningful all in one, and I hope this book can inspire you on all fronts!

*Troy Murrah*

—Troy Murrah
Torrance, California

# Gallery

In the following pages, you'll see photos of my past work. I'll give you a sense of what inspired each piece, without going into too much detail (except for the first piece, which holds a special place in my heart). Final results relied on the materials I had on hand. I owe a lot to these materials for providing the momentum in the process and pushing my creativity along. Hopefully, these pieces will inspire you to grab what you can before it's trashed and create something beautiful.

My mother, Judy Murrah, teaching a quilting class at the old Great Expectations Shop in Houston, Texas, circa the 1970s.

## *Go West, Mary*, 2018 • 36" x 36" (91 x 91cm)
### BROKEN STAR (OR DUTCH ROSE) QUILT BLOCK
*Reclaimed wood, vintage kitchen countertops and cabinetry, wood from a 1930s garage, exterior siding, and brass (framing)*

As this piece was my first, it is extra special to me. In my life, I've been an artist, welder/metal fabricator, and carpenter/craftsman, but I've never been a quilter—so you may wonder how I ended up here, making wooden quilt mosaics. It all began with hearing through the years from my mom, Judy Murrah, "You should do something quilt-related in your art." She was an avid quilter, educator, and VP of Education at Quilts, Inc. She also authored her own how-to series of books, the "Jacket Jazz" books, which taught readers how to sew wearable art jackets based on quilt blocks and traditional sewing techniques.

At the time, I did not feel that her creative suggestion of involving a quilt would meld well with the figurative, multimedia fine art I was doing. It wasn't until after her passing in late 2017 that I figured out a way to do something quilt-related that satisfied me as an artist. In her memory, I decided to build a "quilt" out of reclaimed material I had lying around the studio. My professional life centered on carpentry, metalwork, and designing/building recording studios, and I had a habit of saving interesting leftover material. With the necessary tools already handy, I decided to use this salvaged material to make a wall hanging piece. The result was *Go West, Mary*. It incorporated various laser-engraved elements, including *Mary Poppins*–inspired silhouettes in reference to memories of my mom always singing songs from the movie. It also utilized mostly discarded household/domestic lumber salvaged from a home renovation project—all reminders of home.

To make a long story short, one piece led to another, and I held my first quilt-inspired art show, "Built Quilt," at a local art and wine bar in Long Beach, California, in late 2018. And I'm still doing it! What was initially a one-off memorial for my mom has now turned into my livelihood and enduring art style.

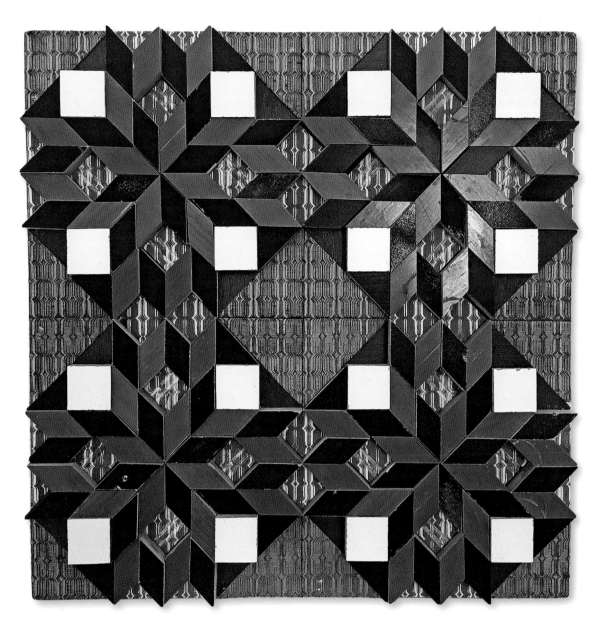

## '70s Ski Party, 2020
## 18" x 18" (46 x 46cm)

### MOTHER'S CHOICE QUILT BLOCK

*Reclaimed wood from a 1980s office desk, black MDF, white particleboard, plywood, Luan wood, yellow pine, and plywood*

Fairly straightforward, this engraved pattern is inspired by a midcentury wallpaper design with white squares representing snow-capped mountains—a place I always like to be. Overall, the color scheme reminded me of a room in my aunt's house from the 1970s.

*A Big Sting Comeback*, 2019 • 84" x 72" (213 x 183cm)
DIAMOND LOG CABIN STAR QUILT BLOCK

*Black masonite, cut-up portrait frames, discarded shelving, MDF
from a commercial set, 2x4s, and kitchen cabinet doors*

The laser engraving was inspired by a vintage tile design. The color scheme was
literally a test to see if red and hot pink would go well with dark natural wood grains. I was
satisfied with this experiment, so I just kept on going until it turned into a seven-footer.

### *Farida's Enchanted Wallpaper*, 2018 • 36¼" x 36½" (92.1 x 92.7cm)
### BURGOYNE SURROUNDED QUILT BLOCK

*Reclaimed wood, wooden dowels, discarded shelving, antique pickled floorboard samples, wall framing,*
*1930s kitchen cabinetry, aged pine, engineered floorboards, brass, and faux wood window molding*

Inspired by castles from fairytale books and vintage wallpaper from my wife Michelle's childhood home,
I also selected the Burgoyne Surrounded pattern for this piece, referencing the many romanticized
battle stories from my childhood. This piece is named after my mother-in-law, Farida.

## *The Strength of a Scorpion Mother*, 2018
## 42½" x 42½" (108 x 108cm)

### LOG CABIN QUILT BLOCK

*Antique wooden tabletop, reclaimed wood from a 19th-century Texas barn, engineered floorboards, and dry-erase board*

Many years ago, I worked as a ranch hand in Texas, where I saw a scorpion with her babies on her back. "How tough that mom has to be," I thought to myself. Most of the symbols in this piece represent toughness and sturdiness (e.g., anvils, sledgehammers)—another homage to the strength of our mothers.

### Doe, A Deer, 2018
### 28" x 28" (71 x 71cm)
**RADIANT (LONE) STAR QUILT BLOCK**

*Discarded shelving, reclaimed countertop, and reclaimed wood*

I was asked to create another piece in memory of my mother for a special exhibit honoring her at the International Quilt Festival, Houston, in 2018. Like Maria from *The Sound of Music*, she had the ability to brighten the day—she also got that haircut at one point, and I've never forgotten!

*Heads Are Important Helmet Hanger, 2019*
38½" x 38½" x 10" (98 x 98 x 25.4cm)
**LONE STAR QUILT BLOCK**

*Acrylic glass, anodized gold aluminum, engineered wood floorboards, vintage school desktop, and steel*

A friend suggested I make a helmet hanger after realizing there weren't many aesthetically pleasing ones out there when he needed one. Helmets should be put on a pedestal.

### *You Make Me Feel*, 2018
### 33" x 33" (84 x 84cm)

**DOUBLE IRISH CHAIN QUILT BLOCK**

*Salvaged primed particleboard, engineered wood floorboards, reclaimed wood from a 1930s garage, and copper (framing)*

Young lovers, jasmine flowers, and Evel Knievel—love and courage seem to go hand in hand, especially in the Western movies that I was watching at the time of this piece's creation.

# Celebrating the Beauty of Reclaimed Materials

In this photo series, I wanted to highlight the reclaimed materials that play such an important role in the process, look, and feel of the pieces in this book. Eventually, all of these materials were incorporated into finished wood mosaics.

### Laying Track, 2020

*Hardwood floorboards, wood from a 1980s dresser, gold spray-painted plywood, anodized gold laminated acrylic glass, blue spray-painted beadboard, plywood, and wood countertop*

### Pocket Full of Change, 2020

*Fluorescent particleboard, anodized gold laminated acrylic glass, and faux wood from a 1970s drawer*

### Mining Town, 2020

*Anodized gold laminated acrylic glass and gold spray-painted pine wood*

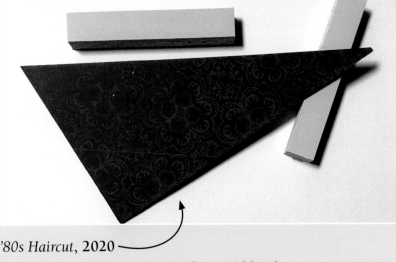

### '80s Haircut, 2020

*Laser-engraved masonite and neon yellow particleboard*

### In the Clouds, 2020

*White acrylic glass and white particleboard*

# PART 1

# Getting Started

Before you dive into the projects, it's important to make sure that you have all the tools you need, understand the terminology used throughout the book, and have a grasp on the basic techniques that pop up many times. You can skim this section before working on your first project and then refer back to it later whenever you need a refresher on a particular topic. There are also some bonus ideas for finishing techniques, aging screws, and other touches you can add to make your pieces personal and unique.

Materials . . . . . . . . . . . . . . . . . . . . . . . . . . . . . . . . . . . . . . . . . . .20

Tools . . . . . . . . . . . . . . . . . . . . . . . . . . . . . . . . . . . . . . . . . . . . . . .22

Techniques, Tips, and Tricks . . . . . . . . . . . . . . . . . . . . . . . . . . . .27

    Using the Patterns . . . . . . . . . . . . . . . . . . . . . . . . . . . . . . . . . .27

    Cutting Specific Shapes . . . . . . . . . . . . . . . . . . . . . . . . . . . . . .28

    Gluing and Assembling . . . . . . . . . . . . . . . . . . . . . . . . . . . . . .30

    Mitering . . . . . . . . . . . . . . . . . . . . . . . . . . . . . . . . . . . . . . . . .30

    Filling . . . . . . . . . . . . . . . . . . . . . . . . . . . . . . . . . . . . . . . . . . .31

    Painting, Distressing, and Staining . . . . . . . . . . . . . . . . . . . .31

    Woodburning and Stenciling . . . . . . . . . . . . . . . . . . . . . . . . .32

    Aging Screws . . . . . . . . . . . . . . . . . . . . . . . . . . . . . . . . . . . . .33

    Hanging Techniques . . . . . . . . . . . . . . . . . . . . . . . . . . . . . . . .33

# Materials

## Reclaimed and Recycled Materials

Most of the material I used for the projects in this book—for all my built quilts—was found, salvaged, or donated to me. The only material I go to the hardware store or lumberyard for is underlayment, plywood, or OSB to be used as the backing boards for the art pieces. (If you're unfamiliar with these terms, see below). Luckily, these are not expensive materials. Everything else is reclaimed off curbsides or from alleyways or left over from construction and carpentry jobs. Anything is fair game—be imaginative and get creative. I have cut up a lot of discarded shelving, wood from a non-functioning piano, remnant floorboards, and thrown-out desks, to name just a few items. This adds to the character, history, and story of each art piece—doing my part to reuse and recycle. Plus, there's the added bonus of cost savings—buying new material can get expensive.

One of the other bonuses of creating this way is finding a wide range of material with interesting and varying finishes, textures, and colors that reduce or eliminate the need to do a lot of staining or surface altering. When

## GLOSSARY OF TERMS

If you're unfamiliar with some of the wood product jargon out there, here are definitions of some of the types of materials you may want to use in your work and that I use throughout the book.

- **Plywood**: This material is basically a sheet form of wood made from gluing multiple thin layers together to make a final thickness. Thicknesses usually range from a thin ⅛" (0.3cm) material up to ¾" (1.9cm), and pieces are generally available in 4' x 8' (122 x 244cm) boards. Plywood is popular in the construction and DIY worlds because of its affordability. In these projects, I often use it as a backing option and sometimes as part of the artistic composition.
- **Luan**: Also spelled Lauan, this is a type of plywood, mainly referring to the thin sheet versions. It's frequently used in the hobby world and sometimes in fine cabinetry making, such as for the bottom panel of a drawer. It comes in a couple of different finishes, and it can take a stain and be painted. I use it often for the small backing boards that I glue my quilt block shapes to before mounting them onto the final backing board, which is usually thicker plywood or OSB.
- **Underlayment**: When I use this term in this book, I'm referring to the plywood form—other underlayments used in the construction world are synthetic and come in rolls. Underlayment is another way to say a thin sheet of plywood, but unlike the Luan mentioned above, it usually doesn't have a nice enough finish to be stained. This is because it's usually installed underneath hardwood flooring and is never seen. It is usually never seen in my work either—I just use it as another backing board option that gets covered up by the built quilt shapes.

- **Particleboard**: Similar to plywood in that it is made by gluing layers, particleboard is manufactured by binding wood chips with an adhesive and pressing flat. It is commonly found in mass-produced, affordable furniture and shelving. I use it a lot because it's a common material I find thrown out by my neighbors. It takes spray paint very well and is great for getting a glossy finish to juxtapose natural wood grains.
- **OSB**: Short for "oriented strand board," OSB is a product like particleboard, manufactured by binding wood strands with an adhesive and pressing flat. OSB is often used on job sites to sheath walls and floors. It has a semi-rough surface and is a great material to use adhesives on. I use it a lot when making wall hangings or furniture involving my built quilts.
- **MDF**: Short for "medium-density fiberboard," the top and bottom surfaces of MDF are very smooth, and its inside is made up of wood fibers, almost like powder, compressed and bound with resin. It can get nasty when cutting, so be sure to wear a mask and eyewear. But it can be fabricated into a large variety of things using wood glue and a nail gun, and it takes paint very nicely after a single coat of primer.
- **Plexiglas®**: This is not wood but rather a popular brand name that has become synonymous with any acrylic glass.

The final collection of materials for the Prosperity Block Shadowbox project included a range of reclaimed items such as hot pink composite wood, anodized gold laminated acrylic glass, and a deteriorating pink and white door.

you're gathering materials for a new project and deciding on the aesthetic, let yourself be inspired by the materials you have, maybe altering the color of just one or two items to create a cohesive collection for your project.

Assuming you have the space for it, collect materials whenever you get the chance. Call friends to see if they have any bits and pieces you can use, or look through your house for a broken shelf that can't be fixed or a dresser that has run its course.

Found and recycled materials can be cleaned by wiping them down with an all-purpose cleaner or industrial degreaser. If it's a piece of furnishing, dismantle it using a screw gun, hammer, or pry bar. It can be fun to destroy a no-longer-useful item with a mind to reuse the materials for something great.

This method of using reclaimed materials is common for traditional quilters—they often use scraps of material and fabric remnants to create their quilts. Resourcefulness is what we're shooting for. Working with what I have inspires me to make color and composition decisions I wouldn't normally have the creative guts to make. I'm pleasantly surprised with how things turn out when I'm forced out of my comfort zone—and I think you will be, too.

## Purchased Materials

If you find that you want or need to purchase new materials for something other than a project's backing board, you need to read the cutting list and instructions and add up the total square footage of wood that you need for each purpose. For example, if you need to cut ten 2" (5.1cm) squares, you could purchase a 2" (5.1cm)–wide strip of wood that is at least 20" (51cm) long, or you could purchase a 4" (10cm)–wide strip of wood that is at least

10" (25cm) long. (But don't get tripped up by nominal lumber sizes—see sidebar below.)

This additive approach is also a good way to ensure that you have enough of a given material for a given purpose before starting a project using leftovers. Because everyone's personal supply of wood looks different, test out a configuration that works for you and your supply.

## NOMINAL AND ACTUAL LUMBER SIZES

Wood is commonly sold in standard widths and thicknesses, such as 1x2, 2x4, etc. The actual width of a 1x2, though, is not 1" x 2" (2.5 x 5.1cm)—it is slightly smaller, at ¾" x 1½" (1.9 x 3.8cm). Here is a quick list of some common nominal lumber sizes with their actual measurements. Nominal lumber is used in a few projects in this book. Don't get confused and try to use a 1x2 to make 2" (5.1cm) squares!

| NOMINAL | ACTUAL | METRIC (ACTUAL) |
|---------|--------|-----------------|
| 1x2 | ¾" x 1½" | 1.9 x 3.8cm |
| 1x3 | ¾" x 2½" | 1.9 x 6.4cm |
| 1x4 | ¾" x 3½" | 1.9 x 8.9cm |
| 1x8 | ¾" x 7¼" | 1.9 x 18.4cm |
| 2x4 | 1½" x 3½" | 3.8 x 8.9cm |
| 2x6 | 1½" x 5½" | 3.8 x 14cm |
| 4x4 | 3½" x 3½" | 8.9 x 8.9cm |

# Tools

The projects in this book require a host of basic workshop tools like a tape measure, hammer, and levels; many simple materials like wood glue, drafting paper, and sandpaper in various grits; and a collection of specific and sometimes specialized tools like a chop saw and table saw to make your life easier and make the projects possible. Read on for explanations on what you'll need and why.

## Paper

How you choose to work with the patterns for these projects will be up to you. You can simply photocopy the patterns onto standard printer paper and work from there; they're designed to work just fine that way. You can redraw the simpler patterns (or even the more complex ones) onto any plain paper of your choice; or you can use a graph or drafting paper to redraw the patterns even more quickly. For large-format projects, you could use larger rolls of drafting paper to recreate the entire design, but it's definitely not necessary. Do what works for you.

## Worktable/Layout Table

Ideally, you want a surface that is 4' x 8' (122 x 244cm); it can be metal or wood. The projects in this book can't be done on your dining room table, unfortunately! You at least want a surface that is strong enough to clamp your pieces to it. Clamping plays a big role in completing the projects and ensuring that they are neat and even. Metal tabletops are durable and easy to clean. If you are not able to use a metal tabletop, a smooth, thick sheet of MDF works well too.

## Table Saw

In all of the projects, this tool sees action first. It is the best tool to use to rip-cut strips of material to specific widths, and you will need to do this for every project in the book, with widths ranging from ¾" (1.9cm) wide to 5" (12.7cm) wide and wider.

## Chop Saw

Just as important as the table saw is the chop saw. This is what you use to make your various shapes—triangles, squares, trapezoids, parallelograms, etc. I use three different sized chop saws, but you only need one. By setting a stop block while using the chop saw, you can

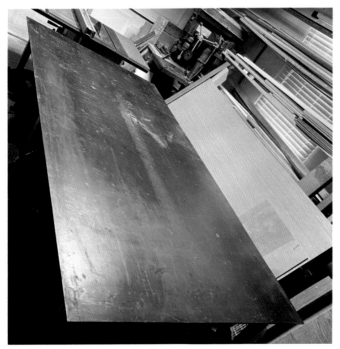

Worktable/layout table

Table saw

Chop saws

quickly cross-cut or angle-cut dozens or hundreds of a repeat shape to the same measurement. For example, you can set the stop at 1" (2.5cm) to feed in a 1" (2.5cm)–wide strip and cross-cut tons of 1" (2.5cm) squares quickly. See more detail about this technique in the Techniques, Tips, and Tricks section.

This is not the norm, but I find that having my chop saws set up right next to my table saw makes the whole cutting process super fast. Don't go so fast that you aren't safe, though!

If you don't have access to a chop saw, these projects are still doable with a miter box. This means all your cuts are done by hand, which isn't a bad thing, it just takes a bit longer to complete. But hey—you'll get some exercise with that arm!

## Circular Saw

This type of saw is primarily used (in this book) to cut down large sheets of plywood or underlayment. Using this saw in combination with a drywall square (or another long straightedge) allows you to cut down your large sheets of material before cutting on the table saw. This tool is especially important for the custom door project, Festival of Stars Door, due to the adjustability of the depth of the blade.

Circular saw

## Grinder (Optional)

I used a 4½" (11.4cm) grinder only once in this book: on the Prosperity Block Shadowbox project, where I decided to use perforated metal. This is not required, and I offer an alternative material to use on that project if you do not have this tool or do not care to work with metal. A grinder comes in handy, though, for anyone who wants to include metal as an art material. It's also useful for cutting off any finishing nails that might be sticking out at the back of your backing board. I advise using a thin, 0.05" (1.27mm) metal cutting disc.

Grinder

## Palm Sander and Sandpaper

The palm sander is an important tool for cleaning or smoothing your material. It is handy any time you want an edge or surface smoothed out, especially right after cutting reclaimed, found materials. It also plays a big part in creating a distressed finish, which I touch upon later. This tool is all about being time-efficient—you can sand by hand, but it takes much longer! The process of truly getting a surface smooth requires multiple grits of sandpaper, starting with a low grit (e.g., 60) and working your way up to a high grit (e.g., 220). In my workshop, I have three different sanders with three different grits loaded at the same time, so I can just grab them quickly. One is plenty, though!

Palm sanders

## Files

Another de-burring and surface-smoothing tool, files are great to round off a top edge of a cut piece. You have more control than with a palm sander because it's a manual hand tool, as opposed to a power tool. I often use files on the edges of painted materials to make them pop more. Remember that files only do their job when moved in one direction. Never try to use a file back and forth like you would sandpaper—you will only damage the teeth. You can purchase several files in a set that give you a variety of options.

## Tape Measure

This is a good all-purpose measuring tool that you'll often use. Make sure yours is at least 8' (245cm) long. That said, you'll actually use squares for a lot of your measuring; these are described below.

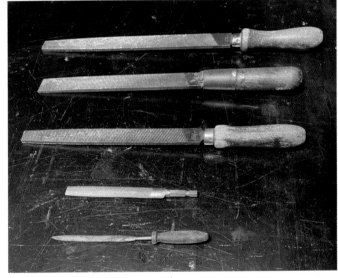

Files

## Squares

I recommend having all four of these types of squares on hand. If you have to choose just a couple, you definitely need a framing square and a combination square. The good news is, unlike chop saws and palm sanders, squares do not normally cost more than fifteen dollars apiece.

- A **drywall square** is a big help when you need to draw a cut line across a large sheet of material, such as plywood. If you don't have one, you can use a long straightedge instead.
- A **speed square** can be used to check if a cut or mounted piece is at a 90° or 45° angle. You can also use this to mark angle measurements.
- A **framing square** (also known as a carpenter's square or steel square) is mainly used to check your 90° angles on larger pieces and is always used to check your final layout frame when the time comes near the end of the project.
- A **combination square** is great for marking strips of material (whether it is a 45° or 90° mark) and setting your blade when using a chop saw. It is also very helpful for precision work.

From top to bottom: drywall square, framing squares, combination squares, speed squares

Assorted clamps

## Clamps

For every project, you need clamps to set up your 90°
layout frames, which you will use to ensure that your
projects' square edges are perfect and true. During
the assembly process, you will clamp down your glued
material while it cures/dries, making sure the pieces don't
shift during the drying process. I prefer the metal, quick-
release bar (sliding arm bar, such as Bessey®) clamps. It is
also crucial to use clamps to clamp down your stop when
cutting on the chop saw. Sometimes you will use up to six
clamps at a time.

## Level

Keep a level on hand for checking the levelness of your
pieces as you work, especially functional pieces like tables.
One will also come in handy when it's time to hang your
work on a wall!

## Nails and Screws

When assembling the built quilt designs in this book,
you will mostly need to use finishing nails and brad nails.
Finishing nails are like common nails, but with smaller
heads meant to sit flush with the wood surface. You can
typically also use finishing nails when assembling backing
hangers and frames around your projects. Brad nails,
or brads, are even smaller, narrower nails that achieve a
similar clean effect. Nails are measured in gauges, such as
16-gauge, which indicates the narrowness of the shaft—
the larger the gauge number, the thinner the nail.

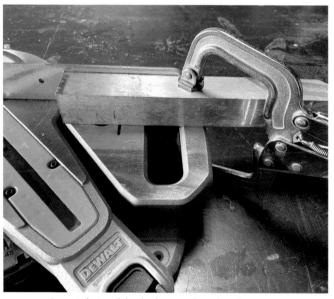

A metal stop block clamped to the chop saw

In this book, screws are mostly used to hang heavier
projects and to assemble the coffee table. Screw widths are
usually designated by numbers, such as #6. Make sure you
purchase the exact screws listed in each materials list.

## Hammer

Use a hammer for driving nails whenever you don't want
or need to use a nailer, described on page 26. In most
applications, though, you should reach for a nailer, not
a hammer.

## Nailers

All these nailers are powered by an air compressor and are listed in order from strongest to weakest—framing nailer, finishing nailer, and brad nailer. You need one or more of these types of nailers to execute most of the projects as cleanly and neatly as possible, though, if necessary, you can make do with just a finishing nailer for most projects.

- The **framing nailer** is mainly used to join larger stock material together (e.g., 2x4s), which you need only for the Pineapple Ice Queen Coffee Table. On a job site, it's used for framing houses and nailing wall studs.
- The **finishing nailer** is for nailing thin 16-gauge nails in various lengths, depending on what you're nailing. Use it to nail down strips or finished blocks when assembling.
- The **brad nailer** is for nailing even thinner 18-gauge nails. It's also used during assembly when you want the nail to be somewhat hidden or you are working with thin, delicate material.

An air compressor with a brad nailer, finishing nailer, and framing nailer

## Cordless Drill and Impact Driver

A cordless drill is used to drill and countersink holes, especially when building the hanging structure for certain projects, and the impact driver is used for actually setting the screws. You can get away with using the drill for both purposes, but it isn't ideal.

## Router

There are basically two different sizes of routers. A regular router is a bit larger than a compact router and is usually used on more heavy-duty projects. The one pictured here, and the one I recommend, is the compact router with a plunge base. It is smaller and easier to handle. These projects are all at a smaller scale, and it is not really necessary to use a bulky two-handed large router. The plunge base allows you to adjust the depth of your router bit, which is very useful. The router bits included in the photo, from top to bottom, are ¼" (0.6cm) and ⅜" (1cm) roundover bits, 1" (2.5cm) and ½" (1.3cm) flush trim bits, a ½" (1.3cm) straight bit (which is in the router), and a ¾" (1.9cm) straight bit. There are plenty more router bits available, but these are the ones I tend to use when making built quilts.

A **roundover bit** has a bearing attached to it, which allows the bit to move along the side of a piece of material while it rounds the top edge. This is a time-saver: instead of using a palm sander to round off the whole length of a top edge, a roundover bit gives a very consistent and even rounded edge by running quickly along the side of your desired wood or material.

A **straight bit** is a very general-use bit for the router. It cuts a groove perpendicular to the router base. I use it mainly to cut into the backs of my small wall hanging pieces so that a screw or nail has a place to go when the piece is ready to hang on the wall.

**Flush trim bits** are probably my most used bit. They also have a bearing that spins at the bottom of the bit's blades.

Router and various bits

This allows the bit to glide along the side of a fixed piece, like a backing frame, while the bit trims away any overhang from the top surface. This creates a flush edge all around.

## Miscellaneous

Information about the following miscellaneous tools is incorporated within the Techniques, Tips, and Tricks section starting on page 27: adhesives (wood glue and industrial-strength adhesive); putty knives and wood filler; painting tools (paintbrushes and rollers); and utility knives.

# Techniques, Tips, and Tricks

## Using the Patterns

The patterns for the projects in this book are based on quilt blocks. Every pattern and pattern piece can be copied straight from the book, no enlargement needed. Some project patterns are small enough that their one pattern page can be copied once, and that's it. Some project patterns are too large to fit on one page in their original, full-size form, but they have been broken down into identical quadrants, so you simply need to make four copies of the single quadrant and assemble them for the full pattern. And a couple of projects are big enough that

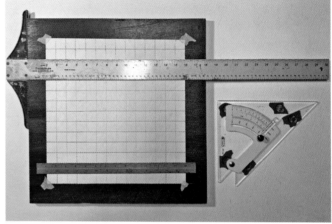

Many of the project patterns are easy to draw yourself with a 1" (2.5cm) grid, but all patterns are provided in the book to photocopy.

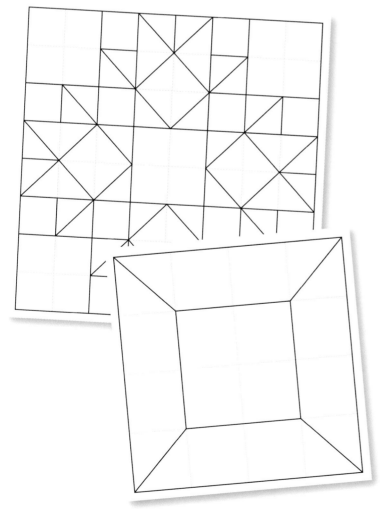

the pattern for the block itself has been split in half, and you need to make a copy of each half and assemble them.

Regardless of the particulars, you don't need a fancy copier—you can copy every pattern in the book at 100% and assemble what you need. Instructions for assembling are included on the pattern page. When assembling a pattern, use a square to ensure you have taped or glued the pattern together true.

Several of the projects in this book are made up of multiple identical blocks; in these cases, the only difference between the blocks is the color scheme you choose to use to create each one—there are no differences in the pattern. You do not need to make copies of more than one full block in these cases, but you can if you wish to plan all your colors ahead of time on paper.

You also have the option of drawing your own patterns. Many of the simpler projects are quite easy to whip up by hand because they follow straightforward measurements, straight lines, and easy angles. Every project pattern is based on either a 1" (2.5cm) or 1½" (3.8cm) grid, so you can start by drawing a grid and then recreating the patterns from there. It's up to you!

# Cutting Specific Shapes

I highly recommend getting into the habit of using a clamped stop block when cutting repetitive shapes. It won't always be possible, but when it is, it can be incredibly helpful to simply clamp a stop block where it needs to go, push your strip of wood into place on the chop saw up against the stop block, and cut without needing to measure every time. I prefer a flat piece of aluminum as a stop, as it's more durable than a piece of wood.

There are four shapes used throughout the projects in this book: rectangles (including squares), triangles, parallelograms, and trapezoids. Here is a quick tutorial on the general technique to use to cut each one. Each time these cuts come up in a project, they are covered in context with relevant measurements, but this is a good introduction to the general idea and can later serve as a reference.

**Important:** When cutting shapes with angle-cuts (that is, the triangles, parallelograms, and trapezoids), always rip-cut strips to the correct height and measure along the straight sides to make the cuts. Do not attempt to cut the angle-cuts/hypotenuses to the exact given measurement. The straight dimensions are always more precise than the given angled side dimensions because these projects are mostly built from interlocking shapes cut from strips of specific widths. If you are cutting from strips of the correct width, your angle-cuts will naturally turn out to be the correct lengths. The angled sides' measurements are given mainly as a reference.

## CUTTING RECTANGLES AND SQUARES

For this example, imagine you want to cut a series of 2" x 10" (5.1 x 25.4cm) rectangles. Rip-cut your strip of material to the correct width—2" (5.1cm). Mark the 10" (25.4cm) line from one end of your strip, set your chop saw to 90°, and place your chop saw blade at the mark. Place your stop against the end of the wood and clamp the stop down (**A**). Then cut the rectangle. To cut more rectangles of the same size, simply slide the wood strip up against the clamped stop each time.

## CUTTING TRIANGLES

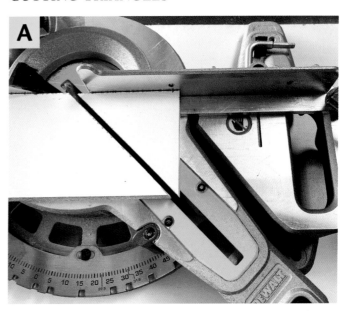

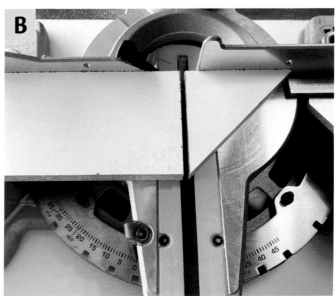

Every triangle in this book is an isosceles right triangle, which simply means it has two equal sides and one 90° angle. For this example, imagine you want to cut a series of triangles that have two 6" (15.2cm) legs. Rip-cut your strip of material to the correct width—6" (15.2cm). Measure and mark 6" (15.2cm) from one end of your strip, draw a 45° line from the opposite corner to your mark, set your chop saw to 45°, and place your chop saw blade at the mark. Place your stop against the end of the wood and clamp the stop down. Cut this first triangle (**A**). Then, mark the second triangle with a straight line, set your chop saw to 90°, push the wood up against the stop, and cut that triangle (**B**). Repeat the sequence to cut more identical triangles—but once you have the stop clamped down, you no longer need to measure and mark each time.

## CUTTING PARALLELOGRAMS

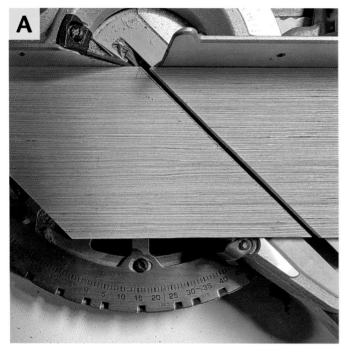

Every parallelogram in this book has 45° angle sides. For this example, imagine you want to cut a series of parallelograms that are 5" (12.7cm) tall (high) and have long sides that are 7" (17.8cm) long. Rip-cut your strip of material to the correct width—5" (12.7cm). Start by setting your chop saw to 45°, cutting a 45° angle at the end of the strip, and discarding the resulting triangle (save it for another project!). Then draw a parallel 45° line 7" (17.8cm) away from the cut edge, place your chop saw blade at the mark, place your stop against the cut edge, and clamp the stop down. Cut the new line to release your first parallelogram (A). To cut more parallelograms of the same size, simply slide the wood strip up against the clamped stop each time.

## CUTTING TRAPEZOIDS

Every trapezoid in this book has 45° angle sides. Cutting trapezoids is a bit like combining cutting triangles and parallelograms. Due to their nature, trapezoids always have two parallel, unequal sides—a long side (often called the bottom or base) and a short side (often called the top). For this example, imagine you want to cut a series of trapezoids that are each 1½" (3.8cm) tall (high), have a long side that is 6" (15.2cm) long, and have a parallel short side that is 3" (7.6cm) long. Rip-cut your strip of material to the correct width—1½" (3.8cm). Start by setting your chop saw to 45°, cutting a 45° angle at the end of the strip (A), and discarding the resulting triangle or wood end (save it for another project!). Then flip the piece over and draw another 45° line, making sure the longest side of the resulting trapezoid is 6" (15.2cm). Place your chop saw blade at the mark, place your stop against the cut edge, and clamp the stop down (B). Cut the new line to release your first trapezoid. To cut more trapezoids of the same size, simply slide the wood strip up against the clamped stop each time, flipping from front to back with every cut.

## Gluing and Assembling

Whenever you are checking measurements in a dry fit or actually doing a final gluing assembly, you need to set up and clamp down a 90° frame corner against which to push your wood backing board. Use this to ensure that your projects' square edges are and remain perfect and true.

Basic wood glue is all you need for gluing wood materials to other wood materials. Especially when assembling the final pieces on the backing board with the wood glue, I recommend pouring the glue into a jar with a resealable lid and applying the glue using a chip brush (a cheap paintbrush). Use dabs and short strokes, leaving gaps between the strokes rather than covering an entire area in glue. This allows space for the glue to spread out when you press your surfaces together.

If you decide to incorporate metal, acrylic glass, or other non-wood materials in your projects, use an industrial-strength multi-surface adhesive. I recommend E6000®. Simply dot it on, and it dries transparent.

When assembling the final blocks onto the large backing board, you should use both glue and a nailer. Glue first, and then, while the glue is still wet, shoot a few finishing nails or brad nails into discreet corners. Use clamps and scrap lumber to hold the blocks against the backing board while the glue dries. This is especially important to do if you are not able to apply any fasteners (this comes up in certain projects).

## Mitering

In some projects, you need to miter ends of wooden strips to create a frame around the art, which is often part of the hanging method. Mitering simply means cutting two pieces at an angle so that they fit together—picture a wooden picture frame where each side is cut at an angle at each corner. When mitering is called for, it is explained in more detail within the project.

It's easy to apply a lot of glue using a brush and an open jar.

Industrial-strength adhesive should be used for materials other than wood.

A final assembly, glued, nailed, and clamped.

A mitered frame around the Prosperity Block Shadowbox project.

# Filling

Sometimes you want or need to treat your artwork's edges or face to smooth them out, both texturally and visually. There are several products that can do the job.

An **automotive body filler**, such as Bondo®, is great for filling large gaps and creating a stronger, more durable surface. In this book, it is occasionally used around the edges of a completed project. Mix per the manufacturer's instructions and quickly spread it on using a putty knife—it dries fast. Once it dries, sand it down with a palm sander. You can paint it, but don't stain it.

**Wood filler** is useful on smaller gaps or when you want to apply a stain later. Most wood fillers are stainable. Though they tend to take a little longer to dry, they're easier to sand away. Applying wood filler is similar to applying automotive body filler, except no mixing is required. It dries slowly and sands away quickly.

**Latex caulking** is mainly used to cover up small finishing nail holes on surfaces you plan to paint. You can apply it with a finger and wipe the excess away with a damp rag. After it dries, paint away!

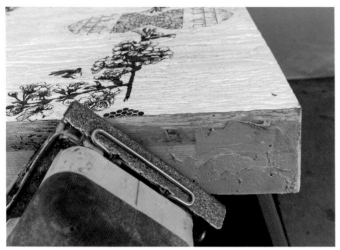
Sanding down automotive body filler.

Freshly applied wood filler.

Latex caulking about to fill a hole.

# Painting, Distressing, and Staining

As I mentioned in the Materials section, I try to use the existing colors of the wood I have on hand. But sometimes, you're going to want to customize a material, whether by changing the color, adding a stain, or distressing.

You can **paint** with both rollers and paintbrushes, depending on what you're painting. For tight spaces, use a small artist's brush, and upgrade to a larger brush when possible. Use a mini (or "weenie") paint roller attached to a roller handle for large, open spaces. Generally, you should apply two to three coats of paint. To achieve a distressed appearance, try rolling on only a single coat of paint and then sanding.

**Spray painting** is great for glossy, stained, and distressed looks. It's fast, and you can often choose a matte or satin finish if glossy isn't what you're going for. I use it mainly to get a bright, glossy surface to contrast the more prevalent

A roller allows you to cover a large surface quickly.

The glossy green here was achieved by spraying three light coats onto some MDF baseboard molding. The bright green pine was sprayed once, then lightly sanded with a fine-grit paper to help the dark grain pop back out.

This pickled, distressed look was achieved by applying and then sanding white spray paint.

## Woodburning and Stenciling

I use a variety of methods, including woodburning, stenciling, and laser engraving, to spruce up the negative space on my built quilts. This is all purely optional and based on personal preference. I enjoy creating wallpaper-esque designs, ornamental patterns, and graphic imagery to add to the artistic sensibilities of my pieces, but you can skip any kind of ornamentation like this and still end up with a vibrant work of art. Here are some details about woodburning and stenciling—I won't cover laser engraving because it requires some large and expensive specialty equipment.

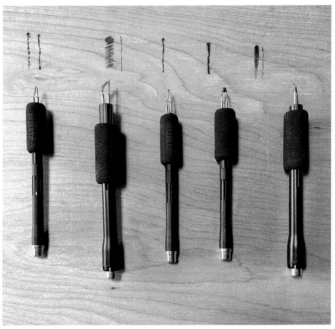

Different tips can create different lines and effects.

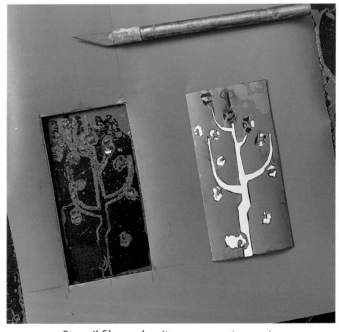

Stencil film makes it super easy to create your own custom stencils.

raw wood surfaces. Follow the manufacturer's instructions for use. Another great thing to do with spray paint is to create a fast stained look or a white pickled, distressed look (as in the Pineapple Ice Queen Coffee Table). Clear coating is a good step to add if you've done a stained or distressed look using spray paint. This protects the faux finish you just created.

And don't forget **staining**, which is a pretty easy way to turn natural wood such as pine into different color tones. Follow the manufacturer's instructions for the product you purchase.

A **woodburning,** or **pyrography, tool** is a great way to quickly add a lot of vivid motifs. Think of these tools as hot pens—instead of ink, you're using heat to mark the wood. My tool of choice is a Razertip® SK. You can purchase inexpensive starter kits at craft stores. There are many different tip options for the tool. With some variety, you can achieve a great deal of detail, shading, and artistic effects like pointillism, almost as if you were drawing with a pencil. Just remember: practice first, burn second.

If you're interested in speed and symmetry, **stencils** are a great way to go. Of course, you can purchase what you need—if you can find it—but making your own stencils allows you to have complete control. Stencils are easy to make with stencil film. I use a product called Oramask® Masking Film. It is easy to cut, easy to draw on, and inexpensive. Draw what you'd like, cut out the design, apply the stencil to the project, and spray paint. For full instructions on creating and using a stencil, see the Prosperity Block Shadowbox project.

## Aging Screws

If you want to age your fasteners or hardware and give them a rusted look, here is the formula for the solution I use. Mix 2 cups (475mL) of hydrogen peroxide, 4 tablespoons (60mL) of white vinegar, and 1½ teaspoons (7.4mL/9g) of table salt in a spray bottle or glass jar. To age screws, soak them in the jar—the longer you leave them, the rustier the look will be. To age a metal surface, spray it with the spray bottle and let the solution sit for ten minutes or more before wiping it off with a damp rag. Experiment until you achieve the look you want.

These are new screws that have been aged for a rustic appearance.

## Hanging Techniques

Among the six hanging projects in this book (this is not including the door or coffee table, which are entire constructions unto themselves), there are five different hanging techniques:

- A backing board with a routed hanging hole (Lattice Square Wall Hanging and Prosperity Block Shadowbox)
- A floating hanger frame (Goose Tracks Woodburned Wall Art)
- A backing frame that can also sit on a desk (Star and Wreath Desk Décor)
- A backing strip (Radiant Lone Star Wood Tapestry)
- A French cleat (Log Cabin Wall Quilt)

Several of these methods are similar to or build upon one another. Each method is explained within its project instructions. To some degree, you could choose to mix and match certain projects with other projects' hanging methods, but if you choose to do so, make sure you double-check both sets of instructions to ensure that nothing goes awry in the execution. You need to be especially careful not to use a less secure or less weight-bearing method for heavier projects.

The floating hanger frame of the Goose Tracks Woodburned Wall Art project.

# PART 2

# Projects

It's time to dive in and make your own stunning built quilts! Each of these wood mosaic projects is based on a different quilt block design. Start simple with one of the first, smaller projects, then, once you've gained some confidence, move on to larger-scale projects, including a full-blown door or coffee table build. You may even want to experiment with applying the quilt block design from one project to a different project's size and structure. Have fun and get cutting!

Lattice Square Wall Hanging . . . . . . . . . . . . . . . . . . . . . . . 36

Prosperity Block Shadowbox . . . . . . . . . . . . . . . . . . . . . . 46

Goose Tracks Woodburned Wall Art . . . . . . . . . . . . . . . . 58

Star and Wreath Desk Décor . . . . . . . . . . . . . . . . . . . . . . 68

Radiant Lone Star Wood Tapestry . . . . . . . . . . . . . . . . . . 78

Log Cabin Wall Quilt . . . . . . . . . . . . . . . . . . . . . . . . . . . . 90

Festival of Stars Door . . . . . . . . . . . . . . . . . . . . . . . . . . . 100

Pineapple Ice Queen Coffee Table . . . . . . . . . . . . . . . . . 114

# Lattice Square Wall Hanging

## 18" x 18" (45.7 x 45.7cm)

This design, great for your first stab at the concept of built quilts, is based on the Lattice Square quilt block. It's a perfect example of "less is more." Sometimes a very simple composition can be just as powerful as a complex layout. This block design uses only two different cut shapes—you'll cut nine squares and thirty-six trapezoids. It's a great block that's simple to make and pleasant to view.

## TOOLS

- ❑ Table saw
- ❑ Chop saw
- ❑ Router with a ¾" (1.9cm) plain bit
- ❑ Tape measure
- ❑ Clamps
- ❑ Framing square
- ❑ Combination square
- ❑ Palm sander
- ❑ Sandpaper in 120, 150, and 220 grits
- ❑ Files
- ❑ Drafting paper or printed pattern (see page 130)
- ❑ Paint tray, roller, and handle
- ❑ Putty knife

## MATERIALS

- ❑ Wood glue
- ❑ Wood filler
- ❑ White house paint
- ❑ Spray paint in desired colors (dark green and bright green shown here)

## CUTTING LIST

| QUANTITY | SIZE & SHAPE | MATERIAL |
|:---:|:---:|:---:|
| 1 | Square: 18½" x 18½", ¼" thick (47 x 47cm, 0.6cm thick) | OSB or plywood (for backing board) |
| 9 | Square: 3" x 3", ¼" thick (7.6 x 7.6cm, 0.6cm thick) | Beadboard or plywood |
| 18 | Trapezoid: 1½" high x 6" long side x 3" short side, ¾" thick (3.8 x 15.2 x 7.6cm, 1.9cm thick) (see diagram) | Pine or similar wood with visible grain |
| 18 | Trapezoid: 1½" high x 6" long side x 3" short side, ¾" thick (3.8 x 15.2 x 7.6cm, 1.9cm thick) (see diagram) | MDF or other smooth, paintable material |

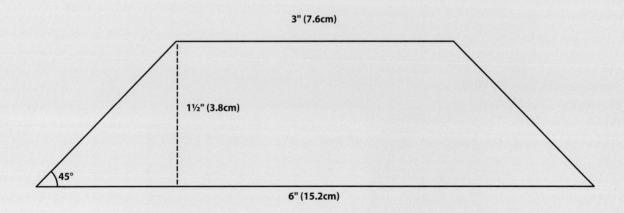

*Shape diagram to scale and actual size.*

# Prep and Collect Materials

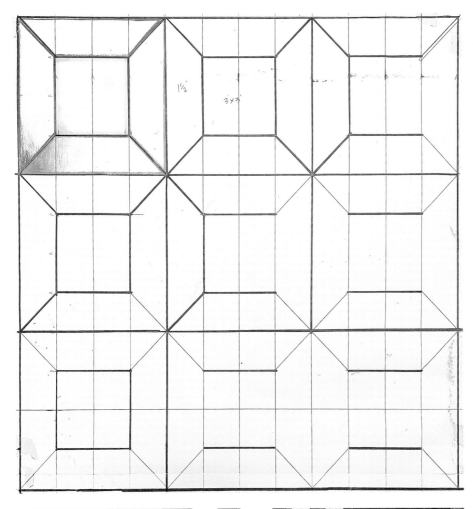

1 **Prep the layout.** Take a look at some existing Lattice Square quilts and the provided diagram of the block's layout. It is an 18" (45.7cm) block based on a 1½" (3.8cm) grid. This will help you get an idea of the scale and help you choose the material you want to use. Recreate the layout diagram on a large sheet of paper by hand, or copy the single unit pattern on page 130 nine times and combine (you can also make just one copy if you prefer).

2 **Hunt for your materials.** Gather and organize the wood and material you want to use. Always make sure you have enough for the total amount needed for each specific shape of the composition. For this piece, I used some old beadboard wood paneling (left), leftover primed MDF baseboard (middle), and some ¾" (1.9cm)–thick pine (right)—long strips of nominal 1x2.

# Paint and Sand

3 **Paint the beadboard.** Roll some white house paint onto the beadboard paneling, painting the entire surface.

4 **Cut the squares.** You can proceed with the other painting steps or cut the beadboard first, as I have done here. Set the table saw fence to 3" (7.6cm) and cut the nine white 3" (7.6cm) squares. If you have chosen to use beadboard as I have, pay attention to the grooves, making sure you cut the squares so that the grooves match up when you do the final layout.

5 **Sand the squares.** Use a palm sander with mild-grit sandpaper, such as 150-grit or 120-grit, to sand the cut edges as well as the painted surfaces of the squares. Sanding the painted surfaces gives the desired aged look.

6 **Spray paint the MDF baseboard.** Apply three light coats to get a consistent, glossy green. I wanted a very classic green for this material. The JD Green color made by Rust-Oleum® was exactly what I was looking for, and it just so happens that the person who commissioned this piece is involved in the agriculture industry—a perfect match.

7 **Spray paint the pine.** To the pine, apply a wash-type spray coat, which is just a single coat lightly applied. This helps some of the grain pop out and serves as a bright green to complement the darker green shade used on the MDF. I tested both of the greens shown in the photo on scrap wood to decide which one I preferred.

## Rip and Cut

8 **Rip strips if necessary.** At this point, all the pieces are painted. As you can see in this photo, though, one of my MDF strips was 3" (7.6cm) wide, so I needed to use the table saw to rip the material into two 1½" (3.8cm) strips. You may or may not need to rip your strips to size, depending on your particular materials.

9 **Cut the first trapezoid angle.** Next, cut the green MDF and pine strips into trapezoids that are 1½" (3.8cm) wide, 6" (15.2cm) long on the long side, and 3" (7.6cm) long on the short side. To start, set your chop saw to 45°, draw and cut a 45° angle at the end of one of your 1½" (3.8cm) strips of material, and discard the resulting wood end.

**10 Cut the second trapezoid angle.** Flip the piece over and draw another 45° line pointing in, making sure the longest side of the resulting trapezoid is 6" (15.2cm). Place your chop saw blade at the mark, making sure the blade's teeth land along the left (outer) side of your line, outside the trapezoid. Place your stop against the cut edge and clamp the stop down. Cut the new line to release your first trapezoid. Repeat until you have cut all eighteen MDF trapezoids and all eighteen pine trapezoids—simply slide the wood strip up against the clamped stop each time, flipping from front to back with every cut. If you have extra material, cut a few extra trapezoids just in case.

## Cut the Backing Board and Glue Down

**11 Cut the backing board.** Cut an 18½" (47cm) square out of plywood or a similar material that is at least ¼" (0.6cm) thick. The final piece will actually be 18" (45.7cm) square, but it is often easier to cut the backing a little oversized and then trim it after you've glued everything down and it has cured. I chose a piece of OSB I had left over from a previous job.

**12 Double-check your cuts.** Double-check your cuts by laying your pieces on the paper layout. Make any necessary adjustments to the size and fit of the pieces.

**13** **Glue.** Once you are confident your cuts are all correct, place the backing board down on your worktable with the bottom left side against a 90° frame corner. Double-check it with a framing square. Then proceed to glue all the cut pieces down onto the backing board using wood glue, starting in the bottom left corner.

# Trim and Clean Up

**14** **Trim the backing.** After the wood glue has dried, place the piece on the table saw. The two sides that were along the clamped-down 90° frame on the layout table should be a true and flush right angle. Place one of those sides against the fence of your table saw. Slide and adjust the fence until the blade's inside edge is right at the edge of the painted piece along a side with excess backing board. Rip the excess material off. Rotate the piece and rip the other part of the excess backing board off.

**15** **Apply wood filler.** Even though all the sides should now be trimmed, straight, and flush, there might be some small spots that need filling, especially since this is the finished edge of the piece—this project doesn't have its edges painted or have any kind of added frame. Spread a basic wood filler along the sides, using a putty knife to apply it as flat and flush as possible.

**16** **Sand the edges.** Once the wood filler has cured, use a palm sander with 150-grit sandpaper to flatten down the bulk of it. Then use fine-grit sandpaper (220-grit or finer) to make it super smooth.

**17** **Sand the corners.** Use fine-grit sandpaper with your hand to lightly sand and de-burr the top corner along the entire outline of the piece.

# Rout a Hanging Hole

**18** **Mark the hole location.** Lay a soft pad, blanket, or cardboard down on your worktable (I used a packing blanket). Put the completed piece on top, face down. Measure and mark the hole location in the middle of the board, 3" (7.6cm) down from the top. (The hole has already been routed in this photo.)

**19** **Rout the hole.** Set your ¾" (1.9cm) plain router bit to make a ⅝" (1.6cm)–deep hole. Place the bit at the mark and slowly rout out the hole. Be careful, hold tight, and don't let the router wander.

# Prosperity Block Shadowbox

The beauty of this block is that it is a very versatile composition. It has the ability to be minimal and straightforward or complex and busy—it just depends on the look you want. I started this block during a time when I was spending many hours looking at the great mosaics of the late Millard Sheets and his studio. He incorporated a lot of gold into his mosaics, and they tend to lean more to the busy side because of all the small cut pieces of ceramic that are composed together to make one of his masterpieces. This influenced my decision-making for this composition. I even created a few figurative woodburnings and stencils based on some drawings I did while researching his work. I don't expect you to make these exact decorative additions, but I will show you the simple steps of making a stencil so that you can add that to your bag of tricks.

Remember, as I walk you through this project, that there are multiple times when you can keep the final outcome of the block much more simplified if you prefer—I point out these moments. On that note, let's start this choose-your-own-adventure block.

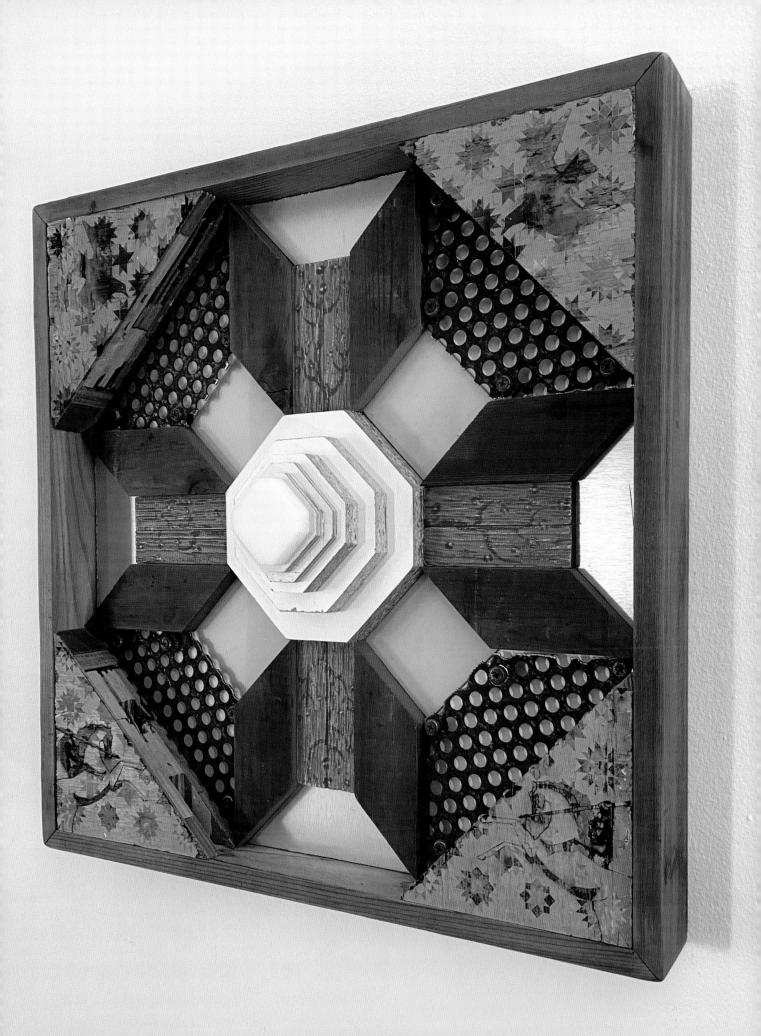

## TOOLS

- ❏ Table saw
- ❏ Chop saw
- ❏ Finishing nailer
- ❏ Brad nailer
- ❏ Air compressor
- ❏ Router with a ¾" (1.9cm) straight bit
- ❏ Grinder with a thin cutoff blade
- ❏ Tape measure
- ❏ Clamps
- ❏ Drywall square
- ❏ Speed square
- ❏ Framing square
- ❏ Combination square
- ❏ Palm sander
- ❏ Sandpaper in 150 and 220 grits
- ❏ Files
- ❏ Drafting paper or printed pattern (see pages 132–133)
- ❏ Utility knife
- ❏ PVC stencil film (such as Oramask)

## MATERIALS

- ❏ Wood glue
- ❏ Industrial-strength adhesive (such as E6000®)
- ❏ Spray paint in desired colors (dusty rose shown here)
- ❏ Perforated metal sheet
- ❏ Nails or brads, 18-gauge 1" (2.5cm), 1¼" (3.2cm), and 1½" (3.8cm) finishing nails
- ❏ Screw, 1½" (3.8cm) #6 wood screw

## CUTTING LIST

*Note: If not specifically provided in this list, the thicknesses of the materials I used were from ⅛"–2" (0.3–5.1cm) thick. You can use any combination of thicknesses you desire. For this project in particular, if you want a similar effect to mine, make sure that the corner triangles are the thickest and that the parallelograms are slightly thicker than the majority of the rest of the shapes.

| QUANTITY | SIZE & SHAPE | MATERIAL |
|---|---|---|
| 1 | Square: 18½" x 18½", ⅝" thick (47 x 47cm, 1.6cm thick) | Any glueable/laminating material (for backing board) |
| 4 | Square: 2¹³⁄₁₆" x 2¹³⁄₁₆" (7.1 x 7.1cm) | Any wood or other material you are comfortable with; I used acrylic glass |
| 4 | Trapezoid: 2¹³⁄₁₆" high x 8½" long side x 2¹³⁄₁₆" short side (7.1 x 21.6 x 7.1cm) (see diagram) | Any wood material |
| 4 | Trapezoid: 2" high x 6" long side x 2" short side (5.1 x 15.2 x 5.1cm) (see diagram) | Any wood material |
| 8 | Parallelogram: 2" high x 4" long sides x 2¹³⁄₁₆" short sides (5.1 x 10.2 x 7.1cm) (see diagram) | Any wood material |
| 4 | Rectangle: 2" x 4" (5.1 x 10.2cm) | Any wood material |
| 4 | Triangle: 6" x 6" x 8½" hypotenuse (15.2 x 15.2 x 21.6cm) | Any wood material |
| 1 | Octagon (with uneven sides): 6" high x 2¹³⁄₁₆" long sides x 2" short sizes (15.2 x 7.1 x 5.1cm) | Any wood material |
| 5 | Mini octagons in diminishing sizes (optional) | Any wood material in pieces smaller than 6" (15.2cm) square |
| 4 | Strip: depth of assembled piece x 19¼", ⅝" thick (depth x 48.9cm, 1.6cm thick) | Any wood material (for frame) |

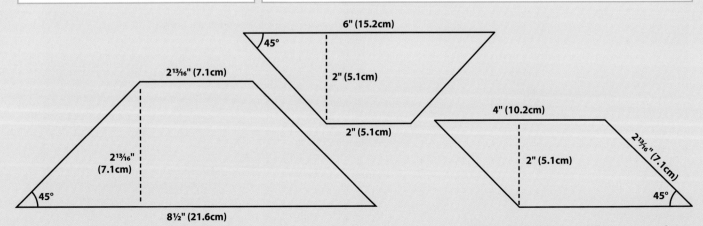

*Shape diagrams to scale but not actual size.*

# Prep and Collect Materials

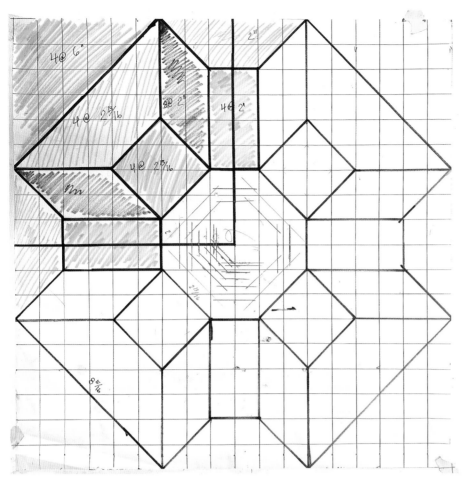

1 **Prep the layout.** This 18" (45.7cm) pattern is based on a 1" (2.5cm) grid and includes triangles, rectangles, squares, parallelograms, trapezoids, and an octagon. The full pattern is made up of four 9" (22.9cm) quadrants, but some of the actual cut pieces (namely, the octagon, the rectangles, and some of the trapezoids) straddle more than one quadrant. Recreate the layout diagram on a large sheet of paper by hand, following a 1" (2.5) grid. Alternatively, copy the large half-square patterns on pages 132 and 133 four times each, combine the halves together to create the four squares, and combine the four squares to assemble the full pattern.

2 **Hunt for your materials.** Gather and organize the wood and material you want to use. Always make sure you have enough for the total amount needed for each specific shape of the composition. For this piece, I used (from left to right) faux wood Formica®, hot pink composite wood, dark wood from a 1930s garage, pink acrylic glass, anodized gold laminated acrylic glass, laminated smooth surface plywood, and a deteriorated pink and white door donated from a family friend.

3 **Rip the strips.** On the table saw, rip assorted materials into the appropriate widths. Rip a 6" (15.2cm) strip of material for the four triangles. Rip 2" (5.1cm) strips of material for the four smaller trapezoids, four rectangles, and eight parallelograms. Finally, rip 2¹³⁄₁₆" (7.1cm) strips of material for the four squares and the four larger trapezoids.

4 **Cut the triangles.** The triangles are isosceles right triangles, which means they have two equal sides (which are 6" [15.2cm]) and one 90° angle. On a 6" (15.2cm) strip, mark and cut a 45° line to get your first triangle. Then, mark the second triangle with a straight line and cut that one. Cut the remaining two triangles the same way.

5 **Cut the parallelograms.** On a 2" (5.1cm) strip, cut the parallelograms using the chop saw. Start by cutting a 45° angle at the end of the strip and discarding the resulting triangle. Draw a parallel 45° line 4" (10.2cm) away from the cut edge, then cut that line to release your first parallelogram. Repeat to cut a total of eight parallelograms, or simply slide the wood strip up against the clamped stop each time.

**6** **Cut the rectangles.** On a 2" (5.1cm) strip, measure and cut the four 2" x 4" (5.1 x 10.2cm) rectangles, one after the other, utilizing a stop to make cutting quick and easy. In this photo, you can see the first three sets of shapes placed on the layout.

**7** **Cut the trapezoids.** First, cut the four smaller trapezoids from a 2" (5.1cm) strip, then cut the four larger trapezoids from a 2¹³⁄₁₆" (7.1cm) strip. Follow the method described in detail in the Techniques, Tips, and Tricks section, summarized here: Cut a 45° line at the end of the strip, then flip the material over, measure the long side of the trapezoid from the edge, draw another 45° line pointing in, and cut. The smaller trapezoid's long side is 6" (15.2cm); the larger trapezoid's long side is 8½" (21.3cm).

**8** **Cut the squares.** On a 2¹³⁄₁₆" (7.1cm) strip, measure and cut the four 2¹³⁄₁₆" (7.1cm) squares, one after the other, utilizing a stop to make cutting quick and easy.

**9** **Cut the central octagon.** First, cut a 6" (15.2cm) square out of your chosen material. Draw crosshairs at the center (extending to all edges) using a combination square or speed square. Make a mark 1" (2.5cm) to either side of all the crosshair lines. Draw 45° angles connecting each mark. Then use the chop saw to cut these angled corners off.

**10** **Cut the mini octagons.** The stack of mini octagons in decreasing sizes is optional. Here's how I went about it. Each new octagon should be of a slightly thinner material and be slightly smaller than the previous octagon in the stack. Follow the same marking and measuring process outlined for the main octagon in step 9, reducing each octagon's height and short sides compared to the previous one. For example, my second octagon is 4½" (11.4cm) square with 1½" (3.8cm) short sides. Make your octagon tower as short or tall as you like.

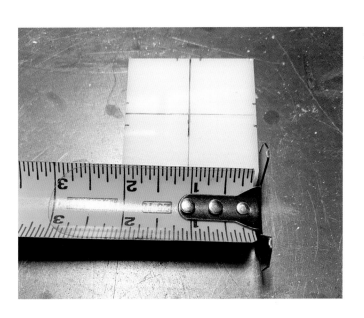

**11** **Make a special final octagon.** I did a total of six octagons, including the main octagon. I thought a thicker peak piece would look more interesting, so my sixth and final octagon is a little special—it's made from a 2" (5.1cm) square of white acrylic glass that is ½" (1.3cm) thick, thicker than the next-smallest octagon. You can use a permanent marker to mark the glass—the lines clean off easily with acetone or denatured alcohol.

# Add Interest with Stencils and Mesh

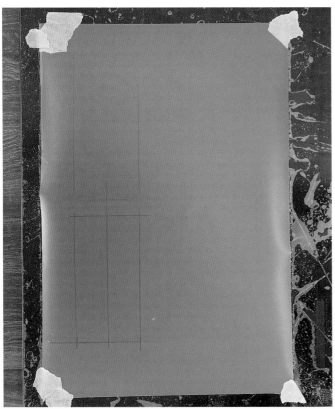

**12** **Outline the stencil.** Tape down a piece of stencil film on a cutting surface. Draw an outline of the shape you are applying the stencil to—in this case, the rectangles.

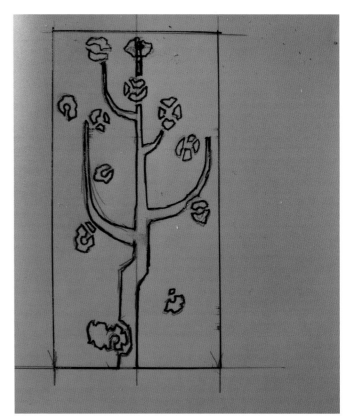

**13** **Draw the design.** Draw the design on the film with a fine-tipped permanent marker. I drew this floral motif inspired by Millard Sheets, as mentioned at the beginning of this project.

**14** **Cut out the stencil.** Use a utility knife to cut out first the design itself, then the stencil border.

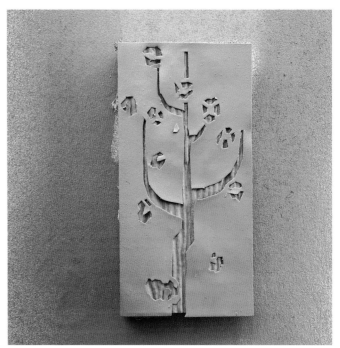

**15** **Apply the stencil.** Place the finished stencil on your piece and spray paint it with a light coat. Let it dry, then peel away the stencil and reuse as desired. For this project, I used the stencil on all four rectangles.

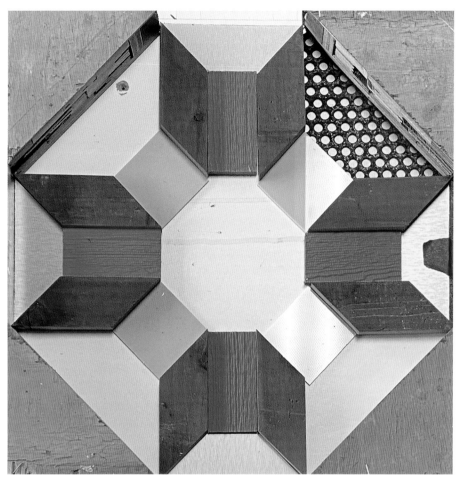

**16** **Check the look.** Another thing you can do is add some rusted perforated metal to the mix. For this project, add it with the larger trapezoids. Insert a piece of your desired material into your dry-fit composition before you cut it, just to make sure you are happy with the effect.

**17** **Cut the metal.** Trace a larger trapezoid onto the metal sheet. Using a grinder with a thin cutoff blade, cut out the metal trapezoid. Repeat for a total of four metal trapezoids.

# Glue and Trim

**18** **Assemble.** Place the backing board down on your worktable with the bottom left side against a 90° frame corner. Double-check it with a framing square. Then proceed to glue and nail (see step 19) all the cut pieces down onto the backing board using wood glue, starting in the bottom left corner. See steps 20 and 21 for instructions on how to attach the central octagon and the stacked octagons—attach the central octagon as part of the main glue-down now, then go back and add the stacked octagons at the end.

**19** **Nail and screw as needed.** If desired, you can screw the metal down with flathead wood screws and cup washers that have been aged using the rusting solution formula given in the Techniques, Tips, and Tricks section. I used 1" (2.5cm) brad nails to secure the four pink triangle corners. These corners are adorned with laser engravings of some drawings I did of sparrows inspired (again) by Millard Sheets' mosaics. They are combined with one of my quilt star pattern designs. Feel free to use the stencil technique or a woodburning tool to add some ornamentation to your four triangle corners.

**20 Attach the wood octagons.** First, glue and screw the main octagon onto the backing board by countersinking right in the middle and countersinking a 1½" (3.8cm) #6 wood screw into it or using some 1½" (3.8cm) finishing nails. Make sure you screw or nail near the middle of the octagon so that the next octagon covers it up. Continue nailing or screwing the rest of the octagons in the stack, except for the final, top octagon, which is attached differently in the next step.

**21 Glue the top octagon.** Apply industrial-strength adhesive to the top octagon if it is acrylic glass, or wood glue if it is wood, and place it on top of the stack. Once you are sure it is centered, use strips of masking tape to hold it in place while the adhesive dries.

**22 Trim and sand.** After the wood glue has dried, use a table saw to trim the excess backing board off so the sides are flush. Then sand and file to clean up the edges. (For more detail about trimming and sanding, see the final steps of the Lattice Square Wall Hanging project.)

# Frame and Hang

**23** **Rip the frame pieces.** It's time to add a frame to the project. Measure the height/depth of the tallest element on your piece, including the backing board. Transfer that dimension over to the setting of the fence on the table saw. Rip your chosen framing wood to the matching height so that the frame is flush with the top surface of the tallest pieces. Rip enough length to complete a frame around the entire block.

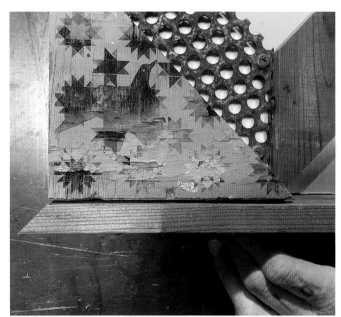

**24** **Cut the frame pieces.** Take exact measurements of the dimensions of the piece from corner to corner—it should be about 18" (45.7cm). Use these measurements plus double the width of your framing wood—in my case, ⅝" (1.6cm)—to cut four frame pieces with a 45° angle at each end that match up in each corner. Give yourself about 1/64" (0.4mm) extra on each cut to be safe.

**25** **Assemble the frame.** Double-check how well the corners meet up around the entire frame. Once you are happy with the fit, glue and nail the frame pieces together using a brad nailer loaded with 1¼" (3.2cm) nails, and then nail them to the backing board using the same nail gun setup.

**26** **Rout a hanging hole.** Flip the piece to the backside to do the routing technique for hanging discussed in the Techniques, Tips, and Tricks section. My backing board, which was an old shelf, already had a channel cut out of it, but I still needed to rout out a deeper hole with a ¾" (1.9cm) straight bit in the middle of the channel for the hanging screw to fit better so the piece would hang more safely.

# Goose Tracks Woodburned Wall Art

**15" x 15" (38.1 x 38.1cm)**

This wall hanging is made mostly from material that had already been colored for previous jobs or projects. It's a more creative and ecologically conscious way to get rid of leftover material I have around the studio from the past, and I highly recommend it. You may even recognize some of these colors from other pieces that are included in this book. Maybe you have some remnants in your workspace that would be a good fit for this block too. During the course of this project, you can also use a pyrography, or woodburning, tool to create the border design. This tool can create everything from very fine lines to large areas of shading with its multiple burning tip options. It's a great tool that can be used on a variety of wood projects.

## TOOLS

- ❑ Table saw
- ❑ Chop saw
- ❑ Finishing nailer
- ❑ Air compressor
- ❑ Tape measure
- ❑ Clamps
- ❑ Framing square
- ❑ Combination square
- ❑ Palm sander
- ❑ Sandpaper in 80, 150, and 220 grits
- ❑ Files
- ❑ Drafting paper or printed pattern (see page 131)

## MATERIALS

- ❑ Wood glue
- ❑ Industrial-strength adhesive (such as E6000®)
- ❑ Spray paint in desired colors (deep blue shown here)
- ❑ Nails or brads, 1" (2.5cm) long

## CUTTING LIST

*Note: If not specifically provided in this list, the thicknesses of the materials I used were from ⅛"–1" (0.3–2.5cm) thick. You can use any combination of thicknesses you desire. For this project in particular, if you want a similar effect to mine, make sure the central squares and triangles and the colorful corner parallelograms are on the thicker side and that the border is the thinnest.

| QUANTITY | SIZE & SHAPE | MATERIAL |
|---|---|---|
| 1 | Square: 15½" x 15½", ⅝" thick (39.4 x 39.4cm, 1.6cm thick) | Particleboard—mine was an old piece of shelving material (for backing board) |
| 48 | Square: 1½" x 1½" (3.8 x 3.8cm) | Light-toned natural or white wood |
| 4 | Square: 1½" x 1½" (3.8 x 3.8cm) | Colored wood, one square each in four different colors |
| 16 | Triangle: 1½" x 1½" x 2⅛" hypotenuse (3.8 x 3.8 x 5.4cm) | Light-toned natural wood |
| 4 | Triangle: 3" x 3" x 4¼" hypotenuse (7.6 x 7.6 x 10.8cm) | Colored wood, one triangle each in four different colors |
| 8 | Parallelogram: 1½" high x 3" long sides x 2⅛" short sides (3.8 x 7.6 x 5.4cm) (see diagram) | Colored wood, two parallelograms each in four different colors |
| 8 | Parallelogram: 1½" high x 3" long sides x 2⅛" short sides (3.8 x 7.6 x 5.4cm) (see diagram) | Aluminum flat bar |
| 4 | Strip: ¾" x 8", ⅜" thick (1.9 x 20.3cm, 1cm thick) | Any wood (for floating hanger frame) |

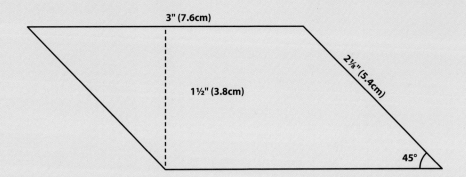

*Shape diagram to scale and actual size.*

# Prep and Collect Materials

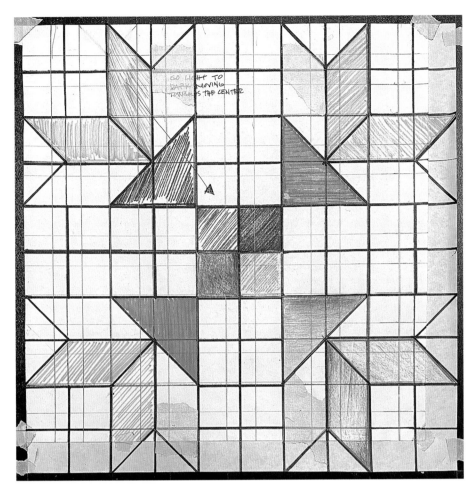

**1 Prep the layout.** This 15" (38.1cm) pattern is based on a 1½" (3.8cm) grid with ten rows and columns and includes triangles, squares, and parallelograms. The full pattern is made up of four quadrants that are each 7½" (19.1cm) squares. Recreate the layout diagram on a large sheet of paper by hand or copy the single quadrant pattern on page 131 four times and combine.

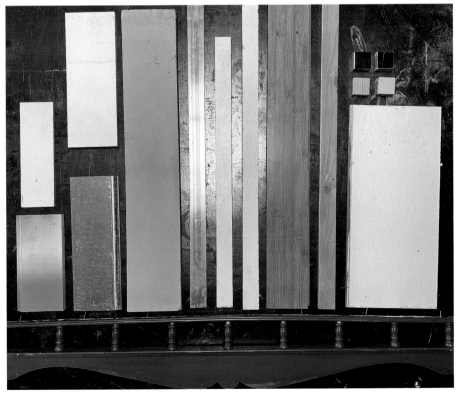

**2 Hunt for your materials.** Gather and organize the wood and material you want to use. Always make sure you have enough for the total amount needed for each specific shape of the composition. My materials included (from left to right) some shelving, a green spray-painted MDF baseboard test piece, gold baseboard that was also used on the Star and Wreath Desk Décor project, an old mustard yellow piece of particleboard from a construction job, ⅛" (0.3cm)–thick aluminum flat bar, two strips of particleboard that were previously ripped to 1½" (3.8cm) wide, bamboo floorboard, bright green pine that was also used on the Lattice Square Wall Hanging project, some small squares left over from previous artwork, part of a 1930s cabinet door, and an old blue oak mirror frame.

**3** **Paint as needed.** For this piece, I used almost exclusively old materials that already had a color treatment applied to them. The only piece that I painted was a 1" (2.5cm)–thick piece from an old shelf, which I sprayed with a glossy, even coat of a deep blue. This became one of the four large colored triangles. You might have to paint or treat a few more pieces of material to get your desired effect. Decide and paint all your pieces now.

**4** **Sand the aluminum.** The only other prep step is to sand the aluminum flat bar with 80-grit sandpaper using the palm sander. Sanding gives the metal a soft, consistent texture and takes away the sheen. Aluminum flat bar is a general type of aluminum stock that can be found at most larger hardware stores.

## Rip and Cut

**5** **Rip the strips.** On the table saw, rip your assorted materials into the appropriate width. Set your table saw fence to 1½" (3.8cm). Rip all the light wood and colored material into strips for making the squares, small triangles, and parallelograms (not all materials pictured here). The ⅛" (0.3cm)–thick natural wood I ripped here is for the border pieces that are woodburned later. I gradually used the thicker white wood as I moved closer to the center of the block. Your pieces' thicknesses may differ—what's important is that the strips are all 1½" (3.8cm) wide. Jump ahead to step 10 if you want to rip the materials for the larger triangles now too.

**6** **Cut the squares.** Use your combination square to mark 1½" (3.8cm) squares on all the appropriate materials. Cut all fifty-two squares on the chop saw, including the forty-eight light-toned squares for the negative space of the design and the four colored squares for the very center.

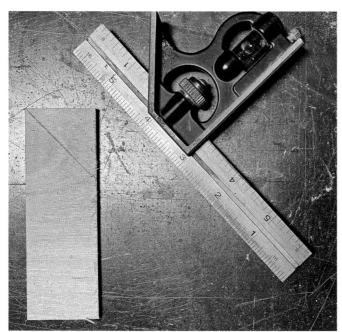

**7** **Cut the small triangles.** The triangles are isosceles right triangles, which means they have two equal sides (which are 1½" [3.8cm]) and one 90° angle. On a 12" (15.2cm) strip of your chosen 1½" (3.8cm)–wide material (or on several shorter strips), mark and cut a 45° line to get your first triangle. Then, mark the second triangle with a straight line and cut that one. Cut the remaining triangles the same way for a total of sixteen triangles. If possible, cut a few extras.

**8** **Cut the parallelograms.** On the appropriate 1½" (3.8cm) strips, cut the parallelograms using the chop saw. Start by cutting a 45° angle at the end of the strip and discarding the resulting triangle. Draw a parallel 45° line 3" (7.6cm) away from the cut edge, then cut that line to release your first parallelogram. Repeat to cut a total of eight wood parallelograms, two in each color—or simply slide the wood strip up against the clamped stop each time. Then repeat to cut a total of eight aluminum parallelograms from the 1½" (3.8cm) aluminum strip. The finishing blade of the chop saw should cut through the aluminum just fine.

**9** **Clean up the aluminum shapes.** Sand and clean up the cut aluminum shapes where needed using fine-grit (220-grit or finer) sandpaper on the palm sander.

**10** **Cut the large triangles.** The four large triangles are also isosceles right triangles, which means they have two equal sides (which are 3" [7.6cm]) and one 90° angle. Grab the four different colors of materials that you've chosen. If you're matching my design, you need blue, dark brown, bright green, and gold. Each raw piece or strip should be 3" (7.6cm) wide; if you need to, rip them to size on the table saw. Then cut the triangles, one of each color, by marking a 45° line with the combination square and cutting on the chop saw.

# Dry Fit and Glue the Border

**11** **Assemble and partially glue.** Cut the 15½" (39.4cm) backing board using the table saw. Place the backing board down on your worktable with the bottom left side against a 90° frame corner. Double-check it with a framing square. Then, without gluing, lay out all your cut shapes onto the backing board, starting with the outside border. Next, place the large triangles, the parallelograms, and the interior squares down, making sure everything fits neatly. Then glue down only the outside border pieces, including the four corner squares (see step 12 image). Leave the assembly intact until the glue has dried.

**12** **Disassemble.** Once the glue has dried, remove all the interior elements so that only the border pieces remain. These are the pieces that you will decorate with a woodburning tool next.

# Woodburn

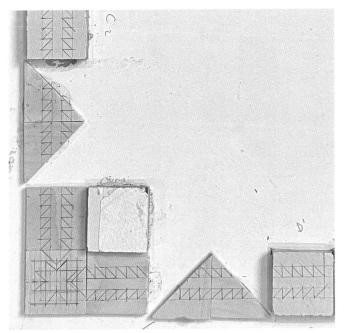

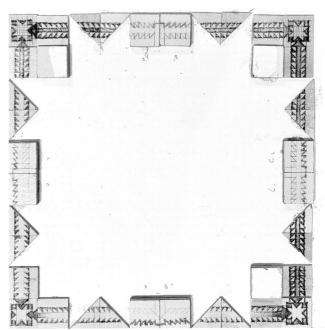

**13** **Select and sketch a design.** First, you need to come up with a border design. I often reference ornamental borders on old illuminated manuscripts, old wallpaper designs, details on real quilts, and ornamental architectural molding. For this project, I chose an old design I adapted from the Wild Goose Chase quilt block. Here you can see my sketches on the wood. Sketch your own design around the entire border as desired.

**14** **Burn.** After sketching, simply trace over the pencil lines with a fine-tipped woodburning tool with the temperature dial at your preferred setting. Different types of wood react in different ways—some may need a hotter heat setting, some may need a cooler setting. Do a few test passes on a scrap piece of wood before starting on the project itself.

## Finish Assembly, Trim, and Hang

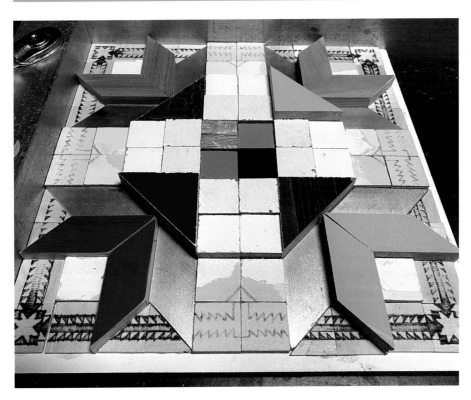

**15** **Finish gluing.** Return the backing board with its completed woodburned border to the layout table. Glue down all the interior pieces using wood glue for the wood and industrial-strength adhesive for the aluminum. Let the glue completely cure.

**16** **Trim off the extra backing board.** Use a table saw to trim the excess backing board off so the sides are flush. Then sand and file to clean up the edges. (For more detail about trimming and sanding, see the final steps of the Lattice Square Wall Hanging project.)

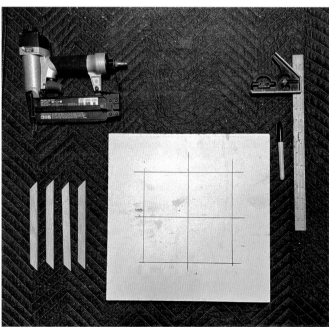

**17** **Create a floating hanger frame.** I call this a floating hanger frame because it makes your piece look like it is floating on the wall. Place a soft pad or blanket down on your work surface to protect the face of your finished project. With a tape measure and combination square, find the center of your backing board and draw an 8" (20.3cm) square. Cut four 8" (20.3cm) strips of ¾" (1.9cm)–wide wood and add 45° miter cuts on each end so that the framing strips fit together within the 8" (20.3cm) square.

**18** **Attach the frame.** With glue and 1" (2.5cm) nails in your 16-gauge finishing nailer or 18-gauge brad nailer, attach the frame strips to the piece using the 8" (20.3cm) square as a guide. Hold your tool at a slight angle, just in case your brads or nails are a little too long, and shoot through the front of your project; this is especially a concern when nailing material that is only ⅜" (1cm) thick. Wait for the glue to dry before hanging.

# Star and Wreath Desk Décor

**14" x 14" (35.6 x 35.6cm)**

Size can be deceiving! While this piece is smaller in size than the previous projects, it's definitely not as simple. This is an intricate, beautiful block. You can modify it in various ways to match your personal taste and make it your own. There are more cuts for this one, which adds to its complexity. But it's a favorite! Once you get the hang of it, you can create variations by playing with different colors. Due to its size and the thickness of the frame, you can also choose to either hang it on a wall or perch it on a desk or other surface.

First, try to find a reference image of a single Star and Wreath quilt block for inspiration. I use all kinds of sources, including books, magazines, and of course, the Internet. Then, once I find an inspiring image, I do my own drawing of the block. This helps me break it down and dissect it to get a good idea about the amount of material I need. While doing my layout drawing, I continue to brainstorm on what colors and materials to use.

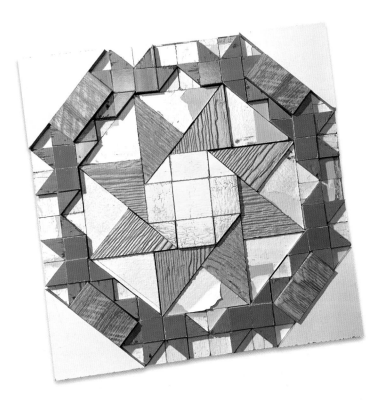

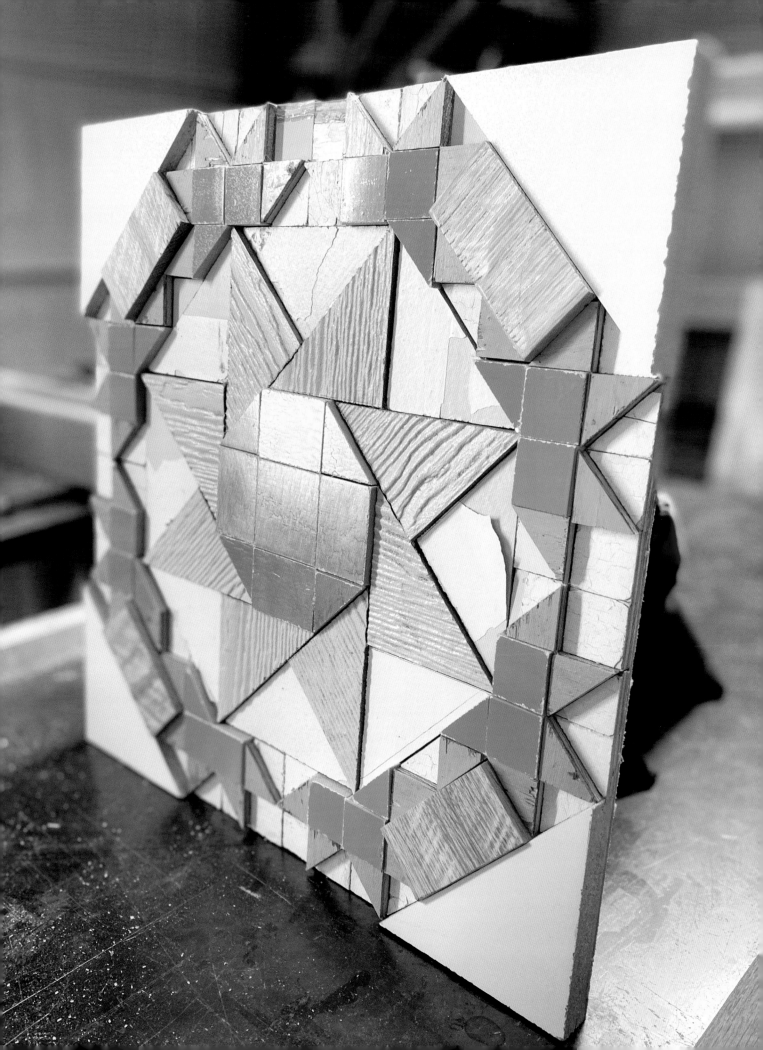

## TOOLS

- ❏ Table saw
- ❏ Chop saw
- ❏ Finishing nailer
- ❏ Brad nailer
- ❏ Air compressor
- ❏ Tape measure
- ❏ Clamps
- ❏ Framing square
- ❏ Combination square
- ❏ Palm sander
- ❏ Sandpaper in 80, 150, and 220 grits
- ❏ Files
- ❏ Drafting paper or printed pattern (see page 140)
- ❏ Putty knife

## MATERIALS

- ❏ Wood glue
- ❏ Wood filler
- ❏ Nails or brads, 18-gauge 1" (2.5cm) brads and 16-gauge 1½" (3.8cm) finishing nails

## CUTTING LIST

*Note: If not specifically provided in this list, the thicknesses of the materials I used were from ³⁄₁₆"–¾" (0.5–1.9cm) thick. You can use any combination of thicknesses you desire. For this project in particular, if you want a similar effect to mine, make the bordering shapes slightly thicker than the central shapes.

| QUANTITY | SIZE & SHAPE | MATERIAL |
|---|---|---|
| 1 | Square: 14" x 14", ¼" thick (35.6 x 35.6cm, 0.6cm thick) | Thin Luan or plywood (for backing board) |
| 4 | Triangle: 2¹³⁄₁₆" x 2¹³⁄₁₆" x 4" hypotenuse (7.1 x 7.1 x 10.2cm) | Light-toned natural wood or other material, same as below material (shown in dark purple in layout diagram) |
| 4 | Triangle: 3" x 3" x 4¼" hypotenuse (7.6 x 7.6 x 10.8cm) | Light-toned natural wood or other material, same as above material (shown in dark purple in layout diagram) |
| 4 | Triangle: 2¹³⁄₁₆" x 2¹³⁄₁₆" x 4" hypotenuse (7.1 x 7.1 x 10.2cm) | White wood or other material, same as below material |
| 4 | Triangle: 3" x 3" x 4¼" hypotenuse (7.6 x 7.6 x 10.8cm) | White wood or other material, same as above material |
| 4 | Rectangle: 2¹³⁄₁₆" x 1⁷⁄₁₆" (7.1 x 3.7cm) | Mid-toned natural wood or other material |
| 8 | Square: 1" x 1" (2.5 x 2.5cm) | White wood or other material |
| 36 | Triangle: 1" x 1" x 1⁷⁄₁₆" hypotenuse (2.5 x 2.5 x 3.7cm) | White wood or other material |
| 16 | Square: 1" x 1" (2.5 x 2.5cm) | Bright color wood, same as below material (shown in dark blue in layout diagram) |
| 8 | Triangle: 1" x 1" x 1⁷⁄₁₆" hypotenuse (2.5 x 2.5 x 3.7cm) | Bright color wood, same as above material (shown in dark blue in layout diagram) |
| 40 | Triangle: 1" x 1" x 1⁷⁄₁₆" hypotenuse (2.5 x 2.5 x 3.7cm) | Mid-toned color wood (shown in light purple in layout diagram) |
| 4 | Triangle: 4" x 4" x 5¹¹⁄₁₆" hypotenuse (10.2 x 10.2 x 14.4cm) | White wood or other material |
| 1 | Square: 2" x 2" (5.1 x 5.1cm) | Gold wood |
| 4 | Rectangle: 2" x 1" (5.1 x 2.5cm) | Gold wood |
| 4 | Triangle: 1" x 1" x 1⁷⁄₁₆" hypotenuse (2.5 x 2.5 x 3.7cm) | Gold wood |
| 4 | Strip: 2½" x 14", ¾" thick (6.4 x 35.6cm, 1.9cm thick) | 1x3 pine (for backing frame) |

# Prep and Collect Materials

1 **Prep the layout.** This 14" (35.6cm) pattern is based on a 1" (2.5cm) grid and includes triangles, squares, and rectangles. The full pattern is made up of four quadrants that are each 7" (19.1cm) square. Recreate the layout diagram on a large sheet of paper by hand, or copy the single quadrant pattern on page 140 four times and combine.

2 **Hunt for your materials.** Gather and organize the wood and material you want to use. Always make sure you have enough for the total amount needed for each specific shape of the composition. I went with some shades of green, natural tones containing a bit of white, and painted white wood—and everything was salvaged from various jobs or donated. My materials included (from left to right) a 1940s cabinet door, green-washed Luan, some exterior siding, a hardwood floorboard, white-washed Luan, and a 1930s kitchen cabinet door.

# Rip and Cut

**3** **Cut the backing board.** You need a clean 14" (35.6cm) square of wood to use as the backing board for this project. Sand the cut edges and set it aside. Unlike other projects in this book, you should start this project with the backing board already cut to the exact final size, rather than trimming excess at the end (you can instead choose to start with excess if you so desire).

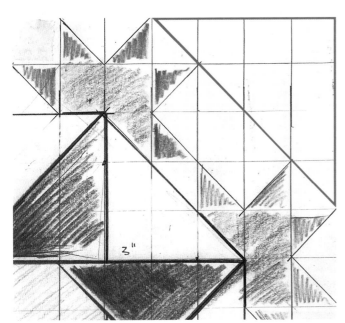

**4** **Rip strips for the corner triangles.** It is time to cut the four large triangles that go at the corners of the piece (indicated here with a bright red outline). Set the table saw fence at 4" (10cm). Rip a 4" (10cm)–wide strip of white material that is at least 10" (25.4cm) long.

**5** **Cut the corner triangles.** The triangles are isosceles right triangles, which means they have two equal sides (which are 4" [10cm]) and one 90° angle. On your prepared 4" (10cm) strip, mark and cut a 45° line to get your first triangle. Then, mark the second triangle with a straight line and cut that one. Cut the remaining triangles the same way for a total of four triangles.

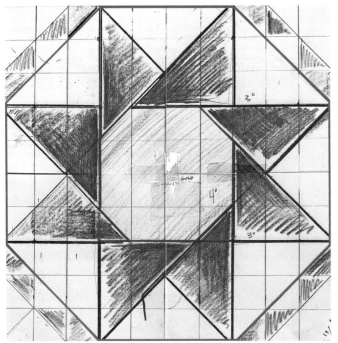

**6** **Prepare to cut the wreath triangles.** Next, cut the ring of triangles that comprises the wreath around the center octagon (the entire wreath is indicated here with a bright red outline). It is made up of eight white triangles and eight colored triangles, four each in two sizes. I chose to use a very pale green exterior siding as the colored wood, which I'm calling light-toned; in the layout diagram, these are the dark purple triangles.

**7** **Rip strips for the wreath triangles.** Rip a $2^{13}/_{16}$" (7.1cm)–wide strip of white material that is at least 6" (15.3cm) long for the smaller white triangles; rip a $2^{13}/_{16}$" (7.1cm)–wide strip of light-toned material that is at least 6" (15.3cm) long for the smaller light-toned triangles. Rip a 3" (7.6cm)–wide strip of white material that is at least 6½" (16.5cm) long for the larger white triangles; rip a 3" (7.6cm)–wide strip of light-toned material that is at least 6½" (16.5cm) long for the larger light-toned triangles.

**8** **Cut the wreath triangles.** Follow the procedure outlined in step 5, using a stop to speed up cutting if desired, to cut four small white triangles, four small light-toned triangles, four large white triangles, and four large light-toned triangles. The small triangles should have two sides that are $2^{13}/_{16}$" (7.1cm), and the large triangles should have two sides that are 3" (7.6cm). Test fit this wreath shape together on your diagram to check the fit (in this photo, you can also see the corner triangles and the rectangles, which we cut next).

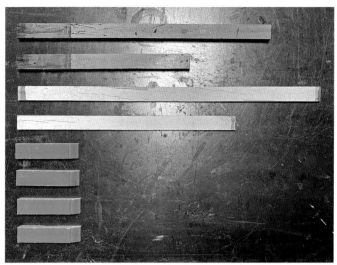

**9** **Rip and cut the rectangles.** Rip a 2¹³⁄₁₆" (7.1cm)–width strip of a mid-toned natural wood that is at least 6" (15.3cm) long. I chose some pickled hardwood floorboards. Use your combination square to mark one (or more) 2¹³⁄₁₆" x 1⁷⁄₁₆" (7.1 x 3.7cm) rectangle on the strip. Cut the rectangles on the chop saw, using a clamped stop to make these repetitive cuts quickly if desired.

**10** **Rip strips for the triangles and squares.** Despite how lengthy the cutting list seems, all of the squares and triangles are simply made from 1" (2.5cm) squares of three different materials—a white, a bright color, and a mid-toned color. The squares are 1" (2.5cm) squares, and the triangles are isosceles right triangles that are halves of the 1" (2.5cm) squares. Rip all necessary strips to 1" (2.5cm) wide. Make sure you have strips totaling at least 27" (69cm) of the white, 21" (54cm) of the bright color, and 21" (54cm) of the mid-toned color—these lengths include 1" (2.5cm) of extra, just in case.

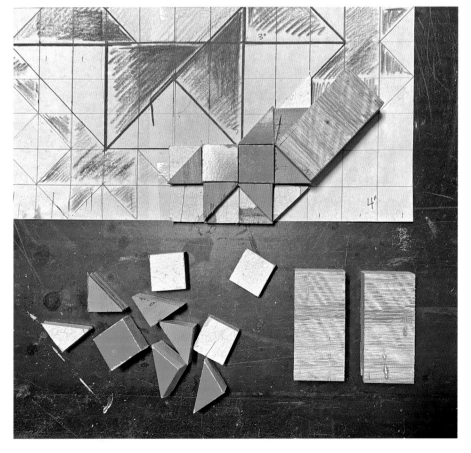

**11** **Cut the squares and triangles.** Following the methods described in steps 5 and 9, cut all the squares and triangles per the Cutting List. At any point, you can start fitting them together on your layout diagram to see how they look and work together.

**12** **Start to glue.** Now that everything except the center gold octagon is cut, it's time to start gluing the pieces down. First, check all pieces for fit on top of the layout diagram. Then transfer all pieces to the backing board, gluing as you go, making sure you have your backing board against a 90° frame corner.

**13** **Prep for the octagon.** There are several ways to make the central octagon. One method is to simply follow the cutting list dimensions to cut individual rectangles, triangles, and squares. This works well if the rest of your assembly was carefully measured. If you are worried about getting a perfect fit, though, use the empty space in the middle of your assembled piece to create a template and proceed from there.

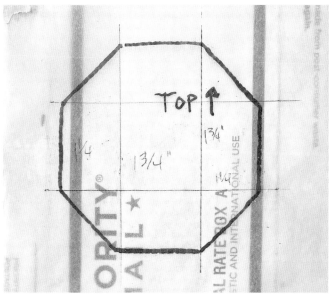

**14** **Make a pattern if desired.** Trace the center octagon from the physical project once the glue has dried. I chose to use nine smaller pieces to create my center octagon. You could also make this octagon from a single full piece of material if you choose, but in my case, the gold molding I wanted to use was not big enough, necessitating the breakdown of the pieces.

**15** **Cut and glue the octagon.** Following the methods described in steps 5 and 9, cut the square, rectangles, and triangles. Once you're happy with how your final octagon turned out, glue it in place.

**16** **Cut the frame pieces.** This backing frame is like the Goose Tracks Woodburned Wall Art project's floating hanger frame but sized instead to fit flush with the art's edge. Take exact measurements of the dimensions of the piece from corner to corner—it should be about 14" (35.6cm) square. Use these measurements to cut four frame pieces with a 45° angle at each end that match up in each corner.

I added a special engraving to my project, which is totally optional, of course!

**17** **Assemble the frame.** Double-check how well the corners meet up around the entire frame. Once you are happy with the fit, glue the frame pieces together and allow them to dry.

**18** **Attach the frame.** Apply dots of glue around the top edge of the newly completed frame and lay the art on top of it. Maneuver the frame where needed to make it as flush to the art's edges as possible. Shoot a few brad nails into hidden spots to tack the piece to the frame. Clamp and allow the glue to cure completely.

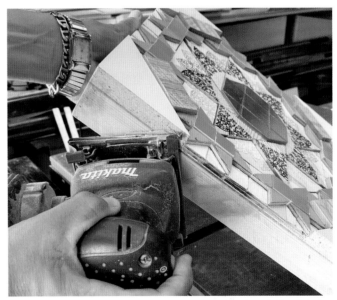

**19** **Trim, fill, and sand.** Once the glue has fully dried, trim the sides just a hair one last time on the table saw to make them super flush. Check all your sides, and, if needed, apply some wood filler with a putty knife. Sand it flat after it dries. You should have a nice and smooth backing frame. This piece is small enough that you could hang it or place it standing on a desk. You can paint the sides or even apply a stain if desired.

# Radiant Lone Star Wood Tapestry

**4' x 4' (121.9 x 121.9cm)**

The Radiant Lone Star (Star of Bethlehem or variation of the Mathematical Star) block is one of my favorites to make as a large-scale wall hanging. If the color choices are right, then the "eye games" begin to play. The piece naturally creates a pulsating or throbbing feel when you look at it, especially when different thicknesses of material are used. It's no wonder that this quilt pattern dates back as far as to the early 1800s (known as the Mathematical Star then) as a symbol of a guiding star for travelers. Since then, it has taken on many variations (with various numbers of points to the star) and names such as Star of Bethlehem, Lone Star (Texas), Blazing Star, Star of the East, Feathered Star… and with the many variations, many special meanings among various groups (including the Amish, Native Americans, and Texans). I made my first in memory of my mother right after her passing, and these types of star quilts are often used to mark other occasions such as weddings and births. The history and cultural significance of this pattern is enough for its own book, but for now, we'll look at its technical aspects and construction.

As complex as it looks, this is actually a fairly simple block composition. The star consists of a total of 600 small 1" (2.5cm)–high parallelograms. This specific piece was commissioned by a patron, who wanted a bee-related engraving to be incorporated; this is why you see the motif in the finished example, as well as cut lines (the piece had to be cut into sections for the engraver). Since most readers won't need a bee motif, skip the engraved pattern and just leave the surrounding area of the star as a solid color. Let's get started!

## TOOLS

- ❏ Table saw
- ❏ Chop saw
- ❏ Circular saw
- ❏ Finishing nailer
- ❏ Brad nailer
- ❏ Air compressor
- ❏ Router with a 1" (2.5cm) flush trim bit (optional)
- ❏ Tape measure
- ❏ Clamps
- ❏ Drywall square
- ❏ Speed square
- ❏ Framing square
- ❏ Combination square
- ❏ Palm sander
- ❏ Sandpaper in 80, 150, and 220 grits
- ❏ Files
- ❏ Drafting paper or printed pattern (see pages 134–135)
- ❏ Paint tray, roller, and handle
- ❏ Paintbrushes in various sizes
- ❏ Putty knife

## MATERIALS

- ❏ Wood glue
- ❏ Industrial-strength adhesive (such as E6000®)
- ❏ Pale yellow house paint (or color of choice)
- ❏ White caulking
- ❏ Automotive body filler (such as Bondo®)
- ❏ Nails or brads, 18-gauge 1" (2.5cm) brads, and 16-gauge 1½" (3.8cm) finishing nails
- ❏ 2 large #10 or #12 screws with anchors

## CUTTING LIST

*Note: If not specifically provided in this list, the thicknesses of the materials I used were from ⅛"–¾" (0.3–1.9cm) thick. You can use any combination of thicknesses you desire. For this project in particular, if you want a similar effect to mine, don't vary the thicknesses of the 600 parallelograms by more than ¼" (0.6cm).

| QUANTITY | SIZE & SHAPE | MATERIAL |
|---|---|---|
| 1 | Square: 48" x 48", ¼" thick (121.9 x 121.9cm, 0.6cm thick) | Sanded plywood (for backing board) |
| 24 | Parallelogram: 5" high x 6⅞" top/bottom sides x 7" left/right sides, ⅛" thick (12.7 x 17.5 x 17.8cm, 0.3cm thick) (see diagram) | Plywood or underlayment (for backing individual parallelogram blocks) |
| 600 | Parallelogram: 1" high x 1⅜" top/bottom sides x 1⁷⁄₁₆" left/right sides (2.5 x 3.5 x 3.7cm) (see diagram) | Any kind of wood or material you are comfortable working with, in any number of colors; I used a variety of shades of natural wood, brown, gold, blue, green, gray, and yellow |
| 4 | Strip: 1½" x 48", ¾" thick (3.8 x 121.9cm, 1.9cm thick) | 1x2 white pine (for backing frame) |
| 1 | Strip: 3½" x 46⅜", 1½" thick (8.9 x 117.8cm, 3.8cm thick) | 2x4 white pine (for backing hanger) |

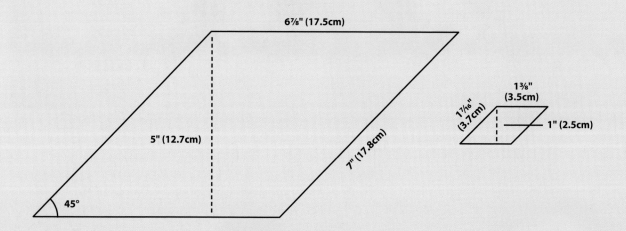

*Shape diagrams to scale but not actual size.*

# Prep and Collect Materials

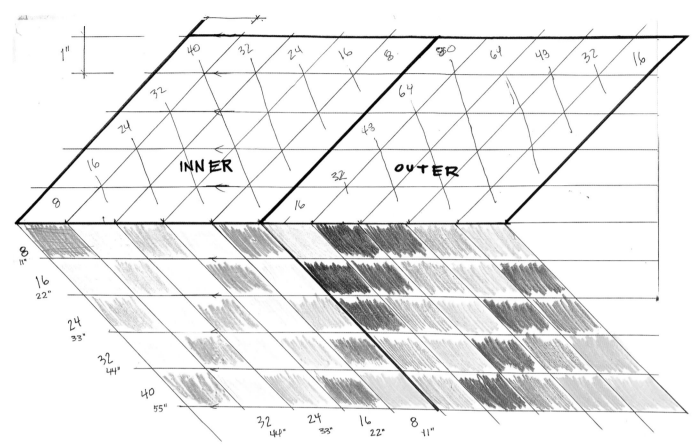

1 **Prep the layout.** This 4' (121.9cm) pattern is based on a 1" (2.5) grid. It is composed of sets of twenty-five small parallelograms glued into twenty-four larger parallelograms, which are then assembled into the star shape. Eight of the larger parallelograms (in one color scheme) make up the center, and the sixteen others (in a different color scheme) comprise the outer ring. Copy each large half-parallelogram pattern on pages 134 and 135 two times, and combine the two pairs to create two full parallelograms. Then mark your own color guide onto each piece as shown here. The numbers indicate how many of each color you will need in total. For final assembly, use the finished project image as an assembly guide.

2 **Hunt for your materials.** Gather and organize the wood and material you want to use. Always make sure you have enough for the total amount needed for each specific shape of the composition. As you can see here, I have some cool tones mixed with some nice natural, warm wood grains. There is also some glossy yellow shelving material that has luckily already been cut into 1" (2.5cm) strips. (This photo doesn't show all of the materials I used, just some of them.) If you're following my color scheme, you want around fifteen to eighteen distinct colors.

# Rip and Cut

3 **Rip the material for the small parallelograms.** All 600 small parallelograms are made from 1" (2.5cm) strips ripped on the table saw. Double-check that you have chosen enough material for each color that you want. In total, you need 600 parallelograms that are 1⅜" (3.5cm) long each on the long side, which is an absolute minimum of 69' (21m) of 1" (2.5cm) strips of the material total. Rip all appropriate materials into 1" (2.5cm)–wide strips now.

4 **Set up to cut the small parallelograms.** Start by cutting a 45° angle at the end of the strip and discarding the resulting triangle. Draw a parallel 45° line 1⅜" (3.5cm) away from the cut edge, place and clamp your stop, then cut that line to release your first parallelogram. The good news is that you only need to mark your cut this one time per strip of material—with your stop clamped on the chop saw, you can just keep feeding in and cutting the strips without measuring.

5 **Cut all 600 small parallelograms.** On the appropriate 1" (2.5cm) strips, cut all the small parallelograms. Get comfortable at your chop saw station, and remember to take breaks if needed. Periodically check your cuts to make sure your stop hasn't moved—it's important that the parallelograms be consistently sized.

6 **Rip and cut the large parallelograms.** The twenty-four large parallelograms serve as backing on which to assemble and glue the sets of twenty-five small parallelograms. Start by ripping 5" (12.7cm)–wide strips that total at least 15' (457cm) long of your ⅛" (0.3cm)–thick underlayment or plywood material. This is just enough to make twenty-four large parallelograms, but cut some extra if you can. Then, follow the same procedure described in step 4 to measure, mark, and cut these shapes: Cut a 45° angle on one end of the strip, measure 6⅞" (17.5cm) from the edge, and draw another 45° line. Set your chop saw blade on the mark, set and clamp your stop, and cut.

# Assemble and Glue

**7** **Arrange the first parallelogram.** Take the twenty-four large parallelograms to your layout table. With your speed square, clamp down your layout frame bars at a 45° angle to match the large parallelograms. Place your first large parallelogram down into and against the frame. Grab all your small parallelograms for the color scheme for your first parallelogram and test the fit, seeing how you like the way your colors are turning out together. You can adjust your color arrangement at this point if you see something working better.

**8** **Start gluing.** Starting with the very tip, glue down the small parallelograms, following your chosen color scheme. For this particular grouping, the point piece, the first piece to be glued, was a gray acrylic glass parallelogram (shown); it needed to be glued down individually using industrial-strength adhesive. For wood, you can simply spread wood glue across the entire surface and place each small wood parallelogram.

**9** **Continue gluing.** Here is what my layout table looks like at this point, with most but not all of my large parallelograms glued. Keep your layout diagram close by to refer to as I have done here. Continue gluing the large parallelograms until you've finished all of them. Try rotating the completed parallelograms to see if you like them oriented differently.

**10** **Don't be afraid to make a change.** When I started experimenting with the final composition, I came across a stronger, more aesthetically pleasing color combination: instead of sticking with my original plan, I put the gold anodized aluminum point in the middle, which creates a center gold star. It doesn't hurt to test out a couple of options before you do the final gluing down of the completed parallelograms to the backing board.

## Make the Backing

**11** **Mark the backing.** Plywood typically comes in 4' x 8' (121.9 x 243.8cm) sheets, which are difficult to cut down on the table saw to the 4' x 4' (121.9 x 121.9cm) size we need for this backing board. So here is a quick way to cut it in half using a circular saw. Lean your sheet against a wall and measure from one edge of the sheet to 48" (121.9cm). At that point, use a drywall square and a permanent marker to draw a 90° straight line down the sheet of wood.

**12** **Prop up the backing.** Prop the backing up on a 2x4 that is on its edge as shown, placing it right at one side of the line you just drew. Propping it like this ensures that the half of the material that is not under the block will fall away from the cut line to avoid pinching the blade and causing it to kickback.

**13** **Cut the backing.** With the board still leaning against the wall and propped up on the 2x4, cut with the circular saw, following the line. Start at the top and let the weight of the circular saw and gravity help you guide it down your sheet of wood.

**14** **Cut the frame.** Now make a 48" (121.9cm) square wooden frame on which to attach the 4' (121.9cm) square backing board. From a 1x2 strip of white pine, cut four frame pieces that are each 48" (121.9cm) long with a 45° angle cut at each end that allows the pieces to match up in each corner. I personally like to make the frame slightly smaller, like the 47⅞" (121.6cm) shown here, and then rout the art perfectly flush with the frame, but sizing to match from the beginning saves you time.

**15** **Assemble the frame.** Glue and fasten each corner with a 16-gauge finishing nailer loaded with a 1½" (3.8cm) nail. Put glue on the top surface of the frame and lay down your 4' x 4' (121.9 x 121.9cm) sheet on top. Secure the board with more nails.

**16** **Rout the edges flush.** If you chose to make the frame slightly smaller, as I described in step 14, you should have a slight overhang of the backing board on all four edges. Let the glue cure, and then rout out the excess with a flush trimming bit so that the backing board is flush with the backing frame. If you chose to make the frame exactly the size of the art from the get-go, skip this step.

**17** **Mark the center crosshairs.** Find the center of the front of the backing board by placing a mark at the halfway point both horizontally and vertically along the edges. Use your drywall square to draw a full line from side to side and top to bottom. This is your center axis from where you start laying out your parallelograms. Keep a framing square handy to help make sure your parallelograms are nailed down straight and square. The broad black lines visible in this photo are factory-made—they usually come on any full sheet of OSB you purchase from the lumberyard. I prefer to make my own marks, even if they happen to align with one of these pre-marked dimensions.

**18** **Start attaching the center parallelograms.** Start attaching the center pieces of the star to the backing board with more brad nails and glue. First, flip the first parallelogram over and apply glue to the backside. Then, place it in the center of the backing board. Put the center (in my case, gold) point right at the center of the crosshair that you drew. Put the edge right along the vertical line. Then, take the next parallelogram and glue it down right below this one. Double-check that both their edges are in line with the vertical axis line.

**19** **Trim as needed.** Continue working your way around the whole star. Try to mainly glue, only nailing when needed, just in case you need to make adjustments throughout the gluing process. Double-check that the parallelograms fit together as seamlessly as possible and on the axis lines. Trim them on the table saw if needed.

**20** **Finish with nails.** Once the star is completed, you can add more brad nails, but try to use a minimal amount. Shoot them in where they are hidden as much as possible.

**21** **Apply a filler along the edges.** The sides should already be pretty clean and flush after using the flush trim router bit (if that's the method you used), but to get the sides even smoother, do a pass over them with automotive body filler (such as Bondo®). Mix per the manufacturer's instructions and quickly spread it on—it dries fast. Once it dries, sand it down with 80-grit sandpaper and then do another pass with 220-grit sandpaper. Next, knock down the corners and the top edges a bit by hand using fine-grit sandpaper.

**22** **Choose your color.** Time to paint! I find that the best way to get the color you want is to get some color swatches from your local home improvement store and place them on your composition to make the decision. You can also often choose the finish of the paint. I went with a semi-gloss pastel yellow, the last color in the row shown.

**23** **Paint around the edges of the star.** Paint by using two different sized tapered brushes and one artist's brush to get in all the nooks and crannies. Carefully apply the paint around all the edges of the star, doing your best not to get any of the paint on your parallelograms.

**24** **Attach the backing hanger.** Before you finish painting, cut a 2x4 to fit snugly into the back of the art. The 2x4 is the support bar that rests on screws in the wall in order to hang the piece. Cut the wood to fit neatly between the 1x2 framing strips on the right and left edges; the length should be around 46⅜" (117.8cm). Apply glue on each of the cut edges and on the 3½" (8.4cm) face of the 2x4 and wedge it between the side framing strips, pushing it all the way up against the top framing strip. Countersink some nails through the side framing strips into the 2x4 and down through the face of the art as well.

**25** **Paint the rest of the backing board.** Use a mini roller to paint the remaining broader, open spaces. To achieve a smooth and even look, you should apply a minimum of two to three coats. Paint one coat, then fill any last nail holes and blemishes with white latex caulking. You can just apply it with a finger and wipe the excess with a damp rag. After the caulking dries, roll on your final coats of paint. Don't forget to roll paint onto the side framing too.

**26** **Hang.** Your piece should look similar to this. It's time to hang! Screw two large #10 or #12 screws into the wall with their appropriate anchors. Check that they are level with each other, lift your piece, and rest the 2x4 hanging bar securely on the screws.

# Log Cabin Wall Quilt

**3' x 6' (91.4 x 182.9cm)**

The large scale of this block pattern may seem intimidating, but don't let that deter you from taking a stab at this fun composition that has plenty of crisscrossing, eye-catching, and colorful patterns. The finished piece is composed of thirty-two 9" (22.9cm) blocks. There is a wide range of layout options for combinations of Log Cabin blocks—it all depends on how and where you place the individual blocks. Here, I'm giving you a design that I feel has a little more depth than the others and plays some good tricks on the eye.

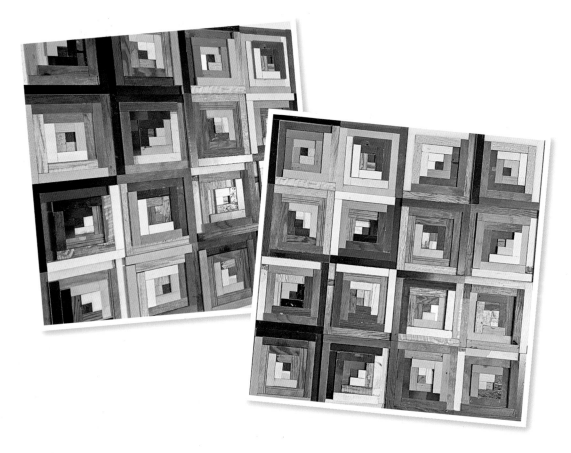

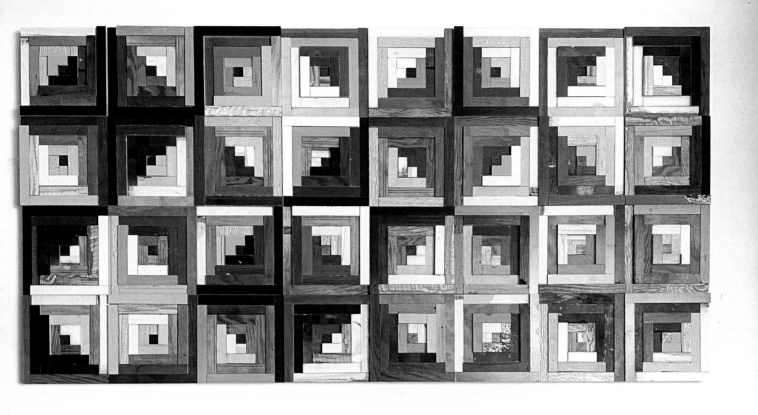
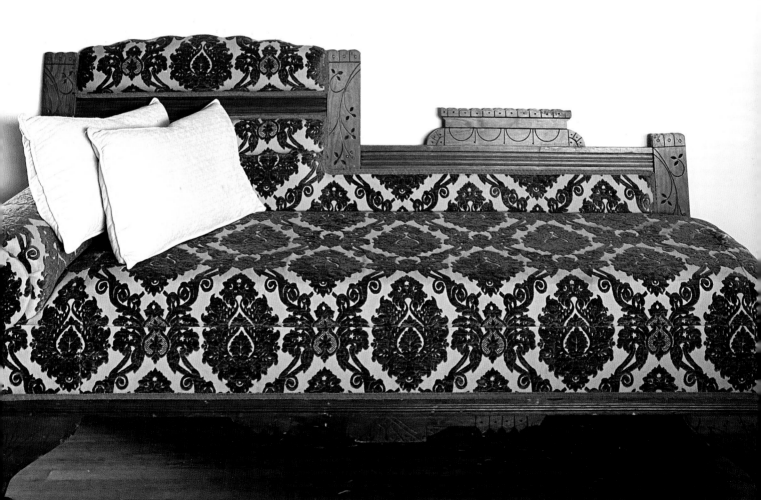

## TOOLS

- ❏ Table saw
- ❏ Chop saw
- ❏ Circular saw
- ❏ Finishing nailer
- ❏ Brad nailer
- ❏ Air compressor
- ❏ Router with a 1" (2.5cm) flush trim bit
- ❏ Tape measure
- ❏ Clamps
- ❏ Framing square
- ❏ Combination square
- ❏ Palm sander
- ❏ Sandpaper in 60 and 150 grits
- ❏ Files
- ❏ Drafting paper or printed pattern (see pages 136–137)
- ❏ Putty knife
- ❏ Power screwdriver and impact driver

## MATERIALS

- ❏ Wood glue
- ❏ Industrial-strength adhesive (such as E6000®)
- ❏ Wood filler
- ❏ Nails or brads, 18-gauge 1" (2.5cm) brads and 16-gauge 1¼" (3.2cm) finishing nails
- ❏ Screws, 3" (7.6cm) #10 wood screws and 1¼" (3.2cm) #6 wood screws

## CUTTING LIST

*Note: If not specifically provided in this list, the thicknesses of the materials I used were from ⅛"–¾" (0.3–1.9cm) thick. You can use any combination of thicknesses you desire.

| QUANTITY | SIZE & SHAPE | MATERIAL |
|---|---|---|
| 1 | Rectangle: 3' x 6', ⅛" thick (91.4 x 182.9cm, 0.3cm thick) | Sanded plywood (for backing board) |
| 32 | Square: 9" x 9", ⅛" thick (22.9 x 22.9cm, 0.3cm thick) | Plywood or underlayment (for backing individual square blocks) |
| 32 | Rectangle: 1" x 9" (2.5 x 22.9cm) | Any dark tone of wood |
| 64 | Rectangle: 1" x 8" (2.5 x 20.3cm) | 32 in any light tone of wood, 32 in any dark tone of wood |
| 64 | Rectangle: 1" x 7" (2.5 x 17.8cm) | 32 in any light tone of wood, 32 in any dark tone of wood |
| 64 | Rectangle: 1" x 6" (2.5 x 15.2cm) | 32 in any light tone of wood, 32 in any dark tone of wood |
| 64 | Rectangle: 1" x 5" (2.5 x 12.7cm) | 32 in any light tone of wood, 32 in any dark tone of wood |
| 64 | Rectangle: 1" x 4" (2.5 x 10.2cm) | 32 in any light tone of wood, 32 in any dark tone of wood |
| 64 | Rectangle: 1" x 3" (2.5 x 7.6cm) | 32 in any light tone of wood, 32 in any dark tone of wood |
| 64 | Rectangle: 1" x 2" (2.5 x 5.1cm) | 32 in any light tone of wood, 32 in any dark tone of wood |
| 64 | Square: 1" x 1" (2.5 x 2.5cm) | 32 in any light tone of wood, 32 in a color not used on any of the above 1" (2.5cm) pieces |
| 2 | Strip: 1½" x 36", ¾" thick (3.8 x 91.4cm, 1.9cm thick) | 1x2 white pine (for backing frame) |
| 2 | Strip: 1½" x 72", ¾" thick (3.8 x 182.9cm, 1.9cm thick) | 1x2 white pine (for backing frame) |
| 1 | Strip: 3½" x 70½", 1½" thick (8.9 x 179.1cm, 3.8cm thick) | 2x4 Douglas fir stud (for backing hanger) |

# Prep and Collect Materials

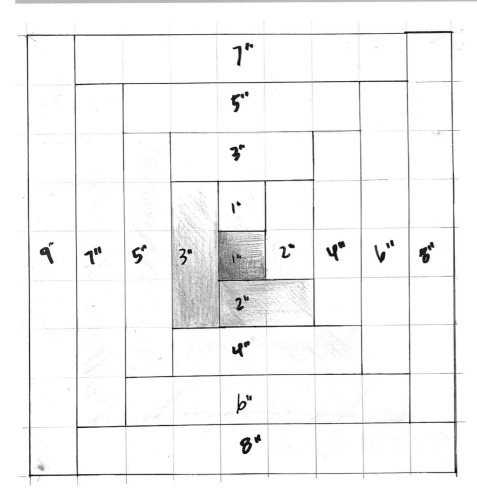

**1** **Prep the layout.** This full pattern is based on a 1" (2.5cm) grid. It is composed of thirty-two 9" (22.9cm) backing board squares that are filled with smaller 1" (2.5cm)–wide rectangles and squares, which are then assembled into one large rectangle. The color scheme is basically half light-toned and half dark-toned wood, with one consistent color used for the center square of each large square. After completing just a few blocks, you'll see how you can easily change up the final layout simply by rotating the large squares. Recreate the layout diagram on a large sheet of paper by hand, following a 1" (2.5) grid. Alternatively, copy the large half-square patterns on pages 136 and 137 and combine the halves together to create one full square. For final assembly, use the finished project image as an assembly guide.

**2** **Hunt for your materials.** Gather and organize the wood and material you want to use. Always make sure you have enough for the total amount needed for each specific shape of the composition. This photo doesn't show all of the materials I used, just some of them—but I used wood from a ton of different sources, including a broken piano,1930s cabinet doors, an old bedroom door, some sample floorboards, some 1980s entertainment center faux grain particleboard, white frosted acrylic glass, and gold spray-painted plywood found in an alley. I left every surface in the condition in which I found it— no painting, staining, or sanding.

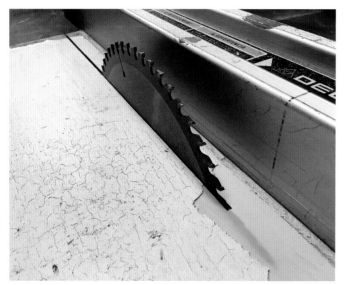

**3** **Rip the strips.** On the table saw, rip the assorted materials for the 544 filler rectangles and squares—not for the 9" (22.9cm) backing squares—into 1" (2.5cm) strips. Set your table saw fence to 1" (2.5cm) and rip away.

**4** **Cut all the filler rectangles and squares.** Following the cutting list, cut all 544 filler rectangles and squares, starting with the thirty-two 1" x 9" (2.5 x 22.9cm) dark-toned rectangles. Take a strip of the material you want to use for your 9" (22.9cm) rectangles to the chop saw. Mark the 9" (22.9cm) line and place the chop saw blade at the mark. Place your stop against the wood and clamp it. Then cut the thirty-two rectangles of this length. Work your way down the cutting list this way, ending with the sixty-four 1" (2.5cm) squares, thirty-two of which should be a unique color from all the rest. Remember that the sets of sixty-four rectangles come in groups of thirty-two dark and thirty-two light.

**5** **Rip and cut the backing squares.** Rip a sheet of ⅛" (0.3cm)–thick plywood or underlayment into 9" (22.9cm) strips. Then use a combination square to mark and cut thirty-two 9" (22.9cm) squares from these strips. Do this either on a chop saw with a stop clamped at the 9" (22.9cm) mark or on the table saw by turning the strips sideways.

## Assemble and Glue the Squares

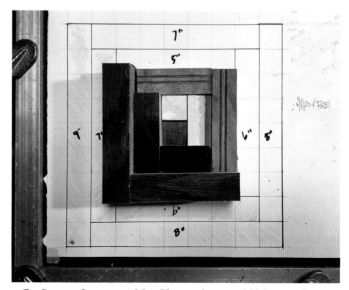

**6** **Set up for assembly.** Clamp down a 90° layout frame to work within and tape down the layout diagram nestled against the frame. Double-check your cuts by placing the pieces on the drawing. If everything looks good, then you can start gluing.

**7** **Glue all the squares and lay out.** One by one, assemble and glue the filler rectangles and squares onto the thirty-two 9" (22.9cm) backing squares. Make sure you follow the photos and illustrations to make each block half light-toned and half dark-toned across the diagonal. Then lay the completed squares out in the eight by four layout, creating two rows of alternating light and dark diamonds.

**8** **Trim squares if needed.** Once you are happy with your arrangement, double-check that the entire assembly is neat and even. If it's not, trim some of the squares as needed on your table saw until the fit of all the squares together is neat.

# Create the Backing Board

**9** **Cut the length first.** Take final measurements of the full assembly; it should be very close to 3' x 6' (91.4 x 182.9cm). Transfer these measurements over to the backing board material to mark the final backing board rectangle. Cut the length of this oversized piece first using a circular saw. Place something under the long side of your material so that the cutoff drops and does not bind on your blade. Also, lower the plate on the saw to lessen the depth of the blade and eliminate any worry of the blade hitting anything. Once you are set up, cut following the 6' (182.9cm) line.

**10** **Rip the width next.** Rip the 3' (91.4cm) width on the table saw. The backing board is now ready for its backing frame.

**11** **Create the backing frame.** Follow the Radiant Lone Star Wood Tapestry project instructions, steps 14 and 15, to create a backing frame from 1x2s that fits your 3' x 6' (91.4 x 182.9cm) backing board. This frame has two short sides and two long sides per the cutting list, rather than equal sides.

**12** **Attach the frame.** Put glue on the top surface of the frame and lay down your 3' x 6' (91.4 x 182.9cm) backing board on top. Secure the board with more nails.

# Create the Hanger and Glue the Design

**13** **Shave the hanger piece.** This project is hung using a French cleat. Here's how it's made. Cut a 2x4 to fit between the two 1x2 left- and right-side backing frame strips—this should be close to or exactly 70½" (179cm). Set the fence on the table saw to 1⁷⁄₁₆" (3.7cm), just a hair under 1½" (3.8cm). Using a ripping blade, run the 2x4 through the saw just to thin its 1½" (3.8cm) thickness down a bit.

**14** **Cut the hanger piece at an angle.** Adjust the table saw blade to 30°. Put the blade in the middle of the 2x4 with the 3½" (8.9cm)–wide face flat on the table saw surface. Cut the board in half.

**15** **Attach the top half of the cleat.** Glue one half of the cleat into the back of the backing frame pushed all the way up against the top framing strip. Make sure the short side is against the backing sheet. Then countersink five screws evenly spaced through the front face of the backing board into the cleat.

**16** **Prepare the bottom half of the cleat.** The other half of the cleat mounts to the wall. Cut this piece down to 24" (61cm) long. Drill and countersink two holes for 10-gauge or larger screws, 16" (40.6cm) apart.

**17** **Screw the cleat into the wall.** Level and screw in the wall-mounted cleat, making sure the short side is against the wall so that the top half of the cleat slides into the angle.

**18** **Glue and nail the design.** Once the glue on the backing cleat is dry, flip the entire backing assembly back over and place it into the 90° setup frame you used in step 6. Glue and nail the 9" (22.9cm) blocks onto the finished backing. Start in the bottom left corner and continue up the left side and along the bottom first. Then work your way across.

**19** **Fill the sides.** When the piece is dry, fill and sand the sides with wood filler to clean them up a bit. After sanding, you can apply a paint or stain, but I left this one raw and natural. It's ready to hang!

# Festival of Stars Door

**18" x 58" (45.7 x 147.3cm) quilt design set into larger door**

This was my second time making the Festival of Stars quilt pattern, but it was the first time I incorporated a built quilt into a door! The Festival of Stars block consists of several star quilt blocks and a variation of pinwheels in between them. This is a great way to make art that is functional. So, let's open some doors!

As you see in the layout diagram, this block is based on three measurements and can be made using a color combination of just three different colors per block (not including the color chosen for the background/negative space). We are sticking to the traditional layout here, but you can stray from tradition when it comes to color combo count.

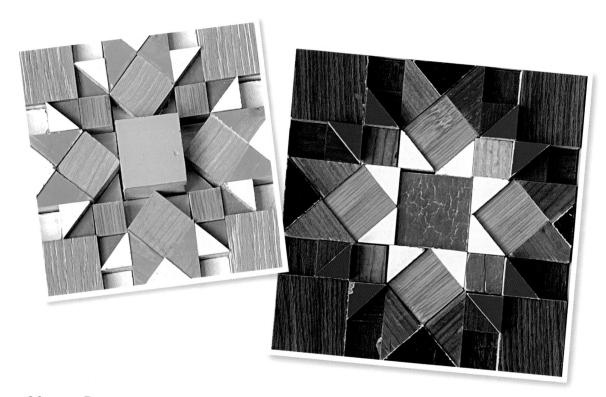

## TOOLS

- ☐ Table saw
- ☐ Chop saw
- ☐ Circular saw
- ☐ Finishing nailer
- ☐ Brad nailer
- ☐ Air compressor
- ☐ Tape measure
- ☐ Clamps
- ☐ Drywall square
- ☐ Framing square
- ☐ Combination square
- ☐ Palm sander
- ☐ Sandpaper in 80, 150, and 220 grits
- ☐ Files
- ☐ Drafting paper or printed pattern (see pages 138–139)
- ☐ Paint tray, roller, and handle
- ☐ Putty knife

## MATERIALS

- ☐ Wood glue
- ☐ Industrial-strength adhesive (such as E6000®)
- ☐ House paint
- ☐ White caulking
- ☐ Automotive body filler (such as Bondo®)
- ☐ Brads, 18-gauge 1" (2.5cm) and 1¼" (3.2cm)

**Cutting List Key:**

- ■ **Red items:** Parts of star blocks
- ■ **Blue items:** Parts of borders between blocks
- ■ **Dark green items:** Parts of pinwheels

## CUTTING LIST

*Note: If not specifically provided in this list, the thicknesses of the materials I used were from ⅛"–1½" (0.3–3.8cm) thick. You can use any combination of thicknesses you desire.

| QUANTITY | SIZE & SHAPE | MATERIAL |
|---|---|---|
| 12 | Square: 9" x 9", ⅛" thick (22.9 x 22.9cm, 0.3cm thick) | Underlayment (for backing individual star blocks) |
| 60 | Square: 2" x 2" (5.1 x 5.1cm) | 48 in any material (for star corners), 12 in any material (for star centers) |
| 48 | Square: 1⁷⁄₁₆" x 1⁷⁄₁₆" (3.7 x 3.7cm) | Any material (for within stars) |
| 144 | Square: 1" x 1" (2.5 x 2.5cm) | Any material (for within stars) |
| 96 | Triangle: 1⁷⁄₁₆" x 1⁷⁄₁₆" x 2" hypotenuse (3.7 x 3.7 x 5.1cm) | Any material (for four tips of stars) |
| 384 | Triangle: 1" x 1" x 1⁷⁄₁₆" hypotenuse (2.5 x 2.5 x 3.7cm) | Any material (for within stars) |
| 12 | Rectangle: 2" x 6", ½" or ¾" thick (5.1 x 15.2cm, 1.3 or 1.9cm thick) | Any material (for top, bottom, and side border strips) (use the same material/color for all border pieces) |
| 4 | Rectangle: 2" x 4", ½" or ¾" thick (5.1 x 10.2cm, 1.3 or 1.9cm thick) | Any material (for middle border strips) (use the same material/color for all border pieces) |
| 20 | Triangle: 1⁷⁄₁₆" x 1⁷⁄₁₆" x 2" hypotenuse, ½" or ¾" thick (3.7 x 3.7 x 5.1cm, 1.3 or 1.9cm thick) | Any material (for border strip points) (use the same material/color for all border pieces) |
| 20 | Triangle: 2" x 2" x 2¹³⁄₁₆" hypotenuse (5.1 x 5.1 x 7.1cm) | Any material, five sets of four of the same color (for pinwheel arms) |
| 20 | Triangle: 1⁷⁄₁₆" x 1⁷⁄₁₆" x 2" hypotenuse (3.7 x 3.7 x 5.1cm) | Any material, five sets of four of the same color (for pinwheel arms) |
| 5 | Square: 2" x 2" (5.1 x 5.1cm) | Any material in various colors (for pinwheel centers) |
| 1 | Rectangle: 18" x 58", ⅛" thick (45.7 x 147.3cm, 0.3cm thick) | Plywood or underlayment (for backing board) |
| 1 | Sized to fit doorway | Hollow-core door |
| 2 | Strip: 1¹¹⁄₁₆" x 18⅞", ⁷⁄₁₆" thick (4.3 x 47.9cm, 1.1cm thick) | MDF flat baseboard (for inlay frame top and bottom) |
| 2 | Strip: 1¹¹⁄₁₆" x 58⅞", ⁷⁄₁₆" thick (4.3 x 149.5cm, 1.1cm thick) | MDF flat baseboard (for inlay frame sides) |
| 1 | Rectangle: 18¾" x 58¾", ⅛" thick (47.6 x 149.2cm, 0.3cm thick) | Underlayment or plywood (for inlay frame backing) |
| 1 | Rectangle: ¾" x 8", ¾" thick (1.9 x 20.3cm, 1.9cm thick) | Pine (for door handle) (optional) |

# Prep and Collect Materials

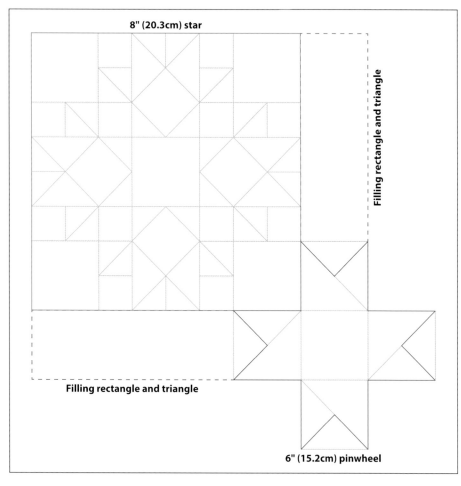

8" (20.3cm) star

Filling rectangle and triangle

Filling rectangle and triangle

6" (15.2cm) pinwheel

**1** **Prep the layout.** This pattern is based on a 1" (2.5cm) grid. It is comprised of six rows of two 8" (20.3cm) star blocks with 2" (5.1cm)–wide rectangles separating them along the sides and a column of 6" (15.2cm) pinwheel blocks between them down the center. The blocks include triangles, squares, and rectangles. Copy the star block and the pinwheel block patterns on pages 138 and 139 and combine them as shown, also carefully drawing in the border rectangles. You likely only need to copy one star block pattern and one pinwheel block pattern to assemble together and use as a guide, but you can copy multiples to recreate the entire assembly if you wish. Alternatively, you can recreate the layout diagram on a large sheet of paper by hand. The color outlines shown here correspond to the three different groupings as listed in the cutting list—stars (red), borders (blue), and pinwheels (dark green).

**2** **Hunt for your materials.** Gather and organize the wood and material you want to use. Always make sure you have enough for the total amount needed for each specific shape of the composition. Ultimately, you have complete creative control over the color placement in your piece. However, you still need to stick with a little bit of color consistency to make the piece work cohesively, so collect colors that work together. My materials included a variety of strips as well as a large collection of extra shapes cut from previous projects in some standard dimensions that proved useful.

# Rip and Cut

3 **Rip and cut the backing squares.** Rip a sheet of ⅛" (0.3cm)–thick underlayment into 8" (20.3cm) strips. Then use a combination square to mark and cut twelve 8" (20.3cm) squares from these strips. Do this either on a chop saw with a stop clamped at the 8" (20.3cm) mark, or on the table saw by turning the strips sideways. I already had some 9" (22.9cm) underlayment squares that didn't get used on the Log Cabin Wall Quilt project, so I used those and trimmed them to size later, as you can see in the photos.

4 **Rip and cut the filler shapes.** Next, rip and cut all the filler shapes for the stars blocks (see cutting list). All the shapes are made from 1" (2.5cm), 1⁷⁄₁₆" (3.7cm), or 2" (5.1cm)–wide strips. After you've ripped the strips, set your stop on the chop saw for each dimension and shape needed and get cutting. This should not be the first project in this book that you make, so instead of exhaustively explaining how to cut each square, rectangle, and triangle here, I instead direct you to the general techniques explained in the Techniques, Tips, and Tricks section.

## Glue the Star Blocks

5 **Verify your arrangement.** Clamp down a 90° layout frame. Nestle one of your 8" (20.3cm)—or 9" (22.9cm), in my case—backing squares tightly into the corner of that 90° frame and begin laying out your shapes using the layout diagram as your guide. Play a little with the colors, experimenting before you start gluing. Then, when you're ready, apply glue to about half of the square.

6 **Glue the star blocks.** Glue shapes one at a time. Start in the bottom left corner and work your way up, staying snug against the clamped frame. Then, work along the bottom row. Next, start filling in the center. After you've covered these areas, brush on more wood glue in the remaining areas and continue adding shapes until the block is done. Complete all twelve star blocks this way.

7 **Neaten as you go.** Use a file to quickly clean any edges before placing the piece on the backing square and remember to check if the assembly is staying true with a framing square or speed square.

8 **Trim and sand.** Place your completed blocks on a flat surface and let them dry. Once they are dry, set your table saw to 8" (20.3cm) and trim the excess backing off if necessary. Then sand the cut edges with a palm sander so they lay nice and flat against the large inlay backing board onto which you will assemble everything later.

9 **Settle your arrangement.** Lay out all twelve completed star blocks and decide where you want each block to go in the two by six arrangement. Look at which colors work best next to each other. Some blocks will look nice together, and some too-similar blocks may need to be separated from one another.

# Cut Border Strips and Pinwheels

**10** **Cut the border strips.** Rip 2" (5.1cm)–wide lengths of your chosen border material, then cut the border strips that go in between each star block (see cutting list for measurements). I ripped my strips from an old faux wood dresser but decided later to paint all the border strip pieces gray for increased contrast with the blocks.

**11** **Cut the border strip triangles.** These triangles are technically included as part of the pinwheel pattern, but in my color scheme, they visually attach to the border strips, as each rectangle has a matching triangle at the end that fits neatly into the pinwheel shape. In this photo, you can see a border triangle, pre-painting, about to be placed into position next to its pinwheel triangle counterpart.

**12** **Rip and cut the pinwheel filler shapes.** Rip and cut all the filler shapes for the five pinwheels (see cutting list). All the shapes are made from 1" (2.5cm), 1⁷⁄₁₆" (3.7cm), or 2" (5.1cm)–wide strips. Rip and cut as described in step 4. Remember—you already cut the twenty end triangles (four per pinwheel) in the previous step (the triangle I'm pointing to in this photo). Keep in mind that to make everything fit nicely, there is always a chance you might have to trim a little bit off some pieces or adjust something when doing the final layout.

## Assemble

**13** **Paint your border if desired.** As I just mentioned, the brown faux wood didn't work for my border pieces, so I had some paint mixed for me based on a color match I came up with using a tone of the doorframe molding where I planned to install this door. I rolled this color onto all the border pieces I cut and fit. Allow to dry before proceeding.

**14** **Put it all together.** Take a rough measurement of the full assembly's total height and width and use a circular saw to cut the plywood or underlayment backing board slightly larger (a couple of inches) than the needed size in both dimensions. (I have given exact dimensions of a "perfect" finished backing board in the cutting list—18" x 58" [45.7 x 147.3cm]—but your project may differ, so to avoid assembling, disassembling, and reassembling the whole thing, sizing up now and trimming down later is a good solution.) Secure the backing board against a 90° clamped frame and assemble the star blocks, the border strips, and the loose pinwheels on top. Take some time to make sure you're happy with how everything fits and the colors of your different pinwheels.

**15** **Glue everything.** Glue the 8" (20.3cm) star blocks down two at a time with their respective border pieces and next-door pinwheels, continually checking for squareness. Work your way from top to bottom as shown.

**16** **Trim.** After all the glue has dried, run the piece through the table saw to remove the excess backing board. Double-check the correct setting of the fence by measuring your piece from the bottom left corner to the top left corner as it's laid out in the clamped 90° frame and doing the same from the bottom left corner to the bottom right corner.

## Create the Inlay Frame and Backing

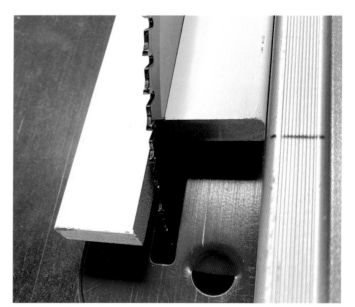

**17** **Measure your assembled piece.** The completed design now needs an inlay frame that fits into the hollowed-out front face of the hollow-core door. First, take the exact final measurements of your built quilt height and width. For the purposes of the instructions, we'll assume that it is the precise 18" x 58" (45.7 x 147.3cm) that the pattern outlines. Also, measure the height of the tallest element of your built quilt—in my case, that's 1¹¹⁄₁₆" (4.3cm).

**18** **Rip the frame strips.** Make the frame by ripping material from a 3" x ⁷⁄₁₆" (7.6 x 1.1cm) MDF baseboard. Rip the MDF to the width of the tallest element measured in the previous step—1¹¹⁄₁₆" (4.3cm). This MDF has a factory-rounded face. That is one edge of the top side of the frame that will stick out from the face of the door. The other edge of the top side that sticks out needs to be knocked down just a little to be rounded as well. Do this with 120-grit sandpaper on your palm sander.

**20** **Assemble the frame.** Double-check your cuts and the overall fit of the frame around the block assembly. When you're satisfied, glue and nail the joints together using a brad nailer. Do not attach them to the assembly at this point—merely assemble the frame itself.

**19** **Cut the frame strips.** The frame is mitered, so the four frame strips need to be cut slightly longer than the height and width of the finished built quilt as measured in step 17 before they are mitered to fit together. Determine your cutting lengths by taking each dimension and adding two times the thickness of your MDF—in this case, $\frac{7}{16}$" (1.1cm). A "perfect" measurement would therefore be $18\frac{7}{8}$" (47.9cm) wide by $58\frac{7}{8}$" (149.5cm) high—though you may want to add an extra $\frac{1}{16}$" (0.2cm) in each dimension to be safe.

**21** **Cut and glue the inlay frame backing.** After the frame joints have had a chance to bond, flip the frame over to the backside. Measure your frame's dimensions (the frame total itself, not the empty space inside the frame). Cut another sheet of underlayment or plywood that is about $\frac{1}{8}$" (0.3cm) smaller on both dimensions than the frame. Based on the "perfect" theoretical height and width of a frame that is $18\frac{7}{8}$" (47.9cm) wide by $58\frac{7}{8}$" (149.5cm) high, this would mean cutting the inlay frame backing sheet to $18\frac{3}{4}$" (47.6cm) wide by $58\frac{3}{4}$" (149.2cm) high. Dab glue around the backside of the frame and then tack the sheet centered to the back of the frame using a brad nailer.

## Prepare the Door

**22** **Check the fit.** Here is the finished inlay frame and the assembled quilt. The assembled quilt should fit neatly into the frame. Dry fit it now and troubleshoot any problems that you find.

**23** **Determine the layout of the door.** Find the exact center of your hollow-core door and decide on the placement of your frame within the door. I prefer the look of a door with a larger border at the bottom, rather than one with the frame centered on all sides. A large bottom border also helps keep the design from getting kicked or damaged while the door is in use. Use your finished inlay frame measurements to mark the placement of the frame on the door, then lay the frame on the door and double-check your marks. Finally, trace the frame while it is in place on the door.

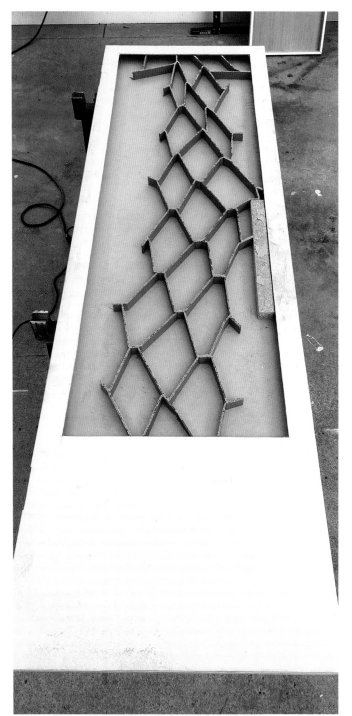

**24** **Cut the hollow for the inlay frame.** Set your circular saw blade's depth shallow enough so that it won't cut all the way through to the backside of the door—you are just cutting a rectangle from the front face of the hollow door, not a hole all the way through the door. Be sure to place the blade right along the inside of the cutline.

**25** **Clean out the hollow.** Remove the rectangular panel you have cut. Here's what the inside of a hollow-core door looks like—just some glue and cardboard strips. Pull out these strips and anything else that might get in the way of the inlay frame being placed neatly inside the hollow—such as the piece of plywood seen in this photo to the right side (which was conveniently already cut with the circular saw while cutting the outline). Then sand the inside surface and the freshly cut edges of the door's face.

# Final Assembly

**26** **Paint the door and inlay frame.** Roll a coat of paint on the front face of the door (where the inlay is going) and the edges. Paint the inlay frame on all sides (the frame only, not the backing board inside it). I matched the color to the border strips of my quilt design. Apply more coats as needed, but keep in mind that a final layer of paint goes on the door in step 29.

**27** **Glue the three pieces together.** Dab glue throughout the inside surface of the door's hollowed-out space and insert the inlay frame. Then dab glue throughout the inside surface of the inlay frame and insert the quilt design.

**28** **Clamp.** Check everything's positioning, and then carefully clamp the door sandwich with scrap material that won't damage the quilt design. Allow to dry.

**29** **Seal the inlay frame.** Seal the inlay frame to the door by putting a small bead of caulking all around the frame. Then wipe it smooth with a wet finger or damp rag. After it has cured, apply a second coat of paint on the door.

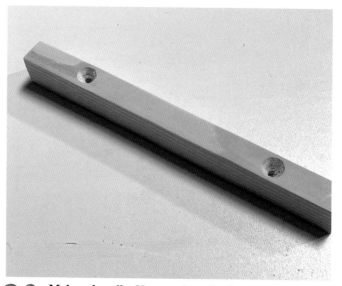

**30** **Make a handle.** You can install a basic doorknob, or you can make a custom one like mine. This minimal handle is made from ¾" x ¾" (1.9 x 1.9cm) pine. It is 8" (20.3cm) long and fits in nicely with the 8" (20.3cm) star block composition. Countersink and screw it onto the door aligned with the third block from the top. Then fill the screw holes with automotive body filler, let dry, sand, and paint.

# Pineapple Ice Queen Coffee Table

**24" x 48" (61 x 121.9cm) quilt design set into larger table**

This final project is the most ambitious. It combines piecing together eight 12" (30.5cm) Pineapple wooden quilt blocks—which are simple enough—with constructing an 18" (45.7cm)–tall wooden coffee table. The instructions are presented in two parts— first, the making of the built quilt, then, the making of the furniture piece.

This idea came out of necessity—we simply needed a new coffee table. I had this furniture design drawn out for a while, but I originally intended for the table frame to be welded steel. Then I spotted some extra 4x4 Douglas fir posts leaning against my studio wall. That prompted me to change the material to wood. I also wanted to try combining a group of Pineapple blocks to see how they looked together. The frame, plus the blocks, plus an acrylic glass topper, and voilà, you get a pretty powerful coffee table that I've named Pineapple Ice Queen.

# Making the Quilt Design

*This tools and materials list is for the quilt design of the tabletop only—see page 121 for the tools and materials list for building the coffee table.

## TOOLS

- ❑ Table saw
- ❑ Chop saw
- ❑ Finishing nailer
- ❑ Brad nailer
- ❑ Air compressor
- ❑ Tape measure
- ❑ Clamps
- ❑ Drywall square
- ❑ Speed square
- ❑ Framing square
- ❑ Combination square
- ❑ Palm sander
- ❑ Sandpaper in 80, 120, and 220 grits
- ❑ Files
- ❑ Drafting paper or printed pattern (see page 141)

## MATERIALS

- ❑ Wood glue
- ❑ Brads, 18-gauge 1" (2.5cm) long

## CUTTING LIST

*This cutting list is for the quilt design of the tabletop only—see page 121 for the cutting list for building the coffee table.

*Note: If not specifically provided in this list, the thicknesses of the materials I used were from ⅛"–1½" (0.3–3.8cm) thick. You can use any combination of thicknesses you desire.

| QUANTITY | SIZE & SHAPE | MATERIAL |
|---|---|---|
| 1 | Rectangle: 24¼" x 48¼", ⅜" thick (61.6 x 122.6cm, 1cm thick) | OSB or plywood (for backing board) |
| 8 | Square: 12¼" x 12¼", ⅛" thick (31.1 x 31.1cm, 0.3cm thick) | Underlayment or plywood (for backing individual square blocks) |
| 32 | Triangle: 4" x 4" x 5⅝" hypotenuse (10.2 x 10.2 x 14.3cm) | 16 in any light-toned material, 16 in any dark-toned material |
| 128 | Triangle: 1" x 1" x 1⁷⁄₁₆" hypotenuse (2.5 x 2.5 x 3.7cm) | 96 in any light-toned material, 32 in any dark-toned material |
| 32 | Trapezoid: 1" high x 6" long side x 4" short side (2.5 x 15.2 x 10.2cm) (see diagram) | Any light-toned material |
| 32 | Trapezoid: 1" high x 5" long side x 3" short side (2.5 x 12.7 x 7.6cm) | Any light-toned material |
| 32 | Trapezoid: 1" high x 4" long side x 2" short side (2.5 x 10.2 x 5.1cm) | Any light-toned material |
| 32 | Trapezoid: 1" high x 3" long side x 1" short side (2.5 x 7.6 x 2.5cm) | Any light-toned material |
| 32 | Trapezoid: 1" high x 5" long side x 2¹³⁄₁₆" short side (2.5 x 12.7 x 7.1cm) | Any dark-toned material |
| 32 | Trapezoid: 1" high x 4¼" long side x 2⅛" short side (2.5 x 10.8 x 5.4cm) | Any dark-toned material |
| 32 | Trapezoid: 1" high x 3½" long side x 1⁷⁄₁₆" short side (2.5 x 8.9 x 3.7cm) | Any dark-toned material |
| 32 | Trapezoid: 1" high x 2¹³⁄₁₆" long side x ¾" short side (2.5 x 7.1 x 1.9cm) | Any dark-toned material |

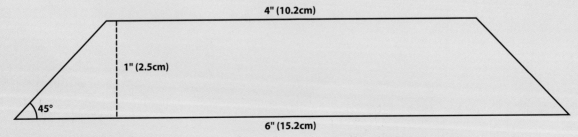

This is the largest trapezoid of the eight different sizes cut. The 1" (2.5cm) height and the 45° angle sides always stay the same, but the lengths of the tops and bottoms change.

*Shape diagram to scale and actual size.*

# Prep and Collect Materials

1 **Prep the layout.** This full pattern is based on a 1" (2.5cm) grid. It is composed of eight 12" (30.5cm) backing board squares that are filled with triangles and trapezoids, which are then assembled into one large rectangle. The color scheme is basically half light-toned and half dark-toned wood. Recreate the layout diagram on a large sheet of paper by hand, or copy the single quadrant pattern on page 141 four times and combine.

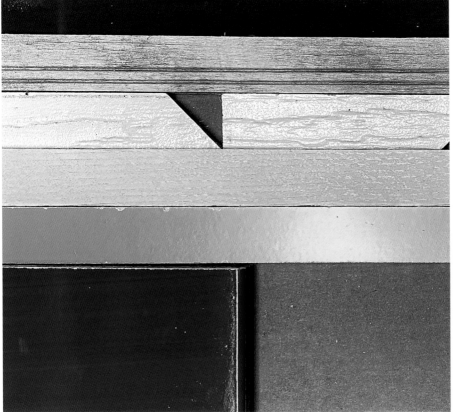

2 **Hunt for your materials.** Gather and organize the wood and material you want to use. Always make sure you have enough for the total amount needed for each specific shape of the composition. For this piece, I stayed rather monochromatic, sticking to whites, grays, blues, and natural wood tones. Feel free to choose your own color breakdown.

# Rip, Cut Shapes, and Dry Fit

**3** **Rip strips and cut shapes.** All the filler shapes (triangles and trapezoids) are cut from 1" (2.5cm) strips except for the 4" (10.2cm) triangles, which are cut from 4" (10.2cm) strips. Start by ripping appropriate materials into strips of 1" (2.5cm) wide and 4" (10.2cm) wide. Then set your stop on the chop saw for each dimension and shape needed and get cutting. This should not be the first project in this book that you make, so instead of exhaustively explaining how to cut each individual shape here, I instead direct you to the general techniques explained in the Techniques, Tips, and Tricks section.

**4** **Dry fit.** After you have cut all your filler shapes, lay them out into 12" (30.5cm) blocks with a 90° corner frame as a guide placed in the bottom left corner. You will make two each of four different block compositions for a total of eight blocks. Use the layout diagram to double-check that all pieces fit and no trimming is necessary. Keep your pieces organized to speed up the assembly process. I usually use old glass jars, empty coffee cans, cardboard boxes, buckets, and the like.

**5** **Tweak as needed.** While laying out the blocks, you might find little tweaks to make here and there. For example, I realized these purple pieces might pop out a little more if I filed the edges to allow some of the white underneath the purple to show.

**6** **Finalize your composition.** Once you are happy with your four compositions (one of mine is shown here), make sure you have enough cut filler shapes to make a matching partner for each of the four.

**7** **Cut the block backing squares.** Rip a 12¼" (31.1cm) strip of underlayment or plywood on your table saw, and then cut your eight 12¼" (31.1cm) individual backing squares, one for each block.

## Assemble

**8** **Glue the blocks.** Clamp down your 90° frame and slide a backing square against the frame. Begin gluing the pieces of your block, starting in the bottom left corner. Continue by gluing the two sides that touch the frame. Work your way toward the opposite corner. After the block is glued, check the trueness of this opposite corner with a square. Repeat until you have glued all eight blocks.

**9** **Trim the blocks.** After the glue has dried, trim the slightly oversized blocks down to 12" (30.5cm) on the table saw.

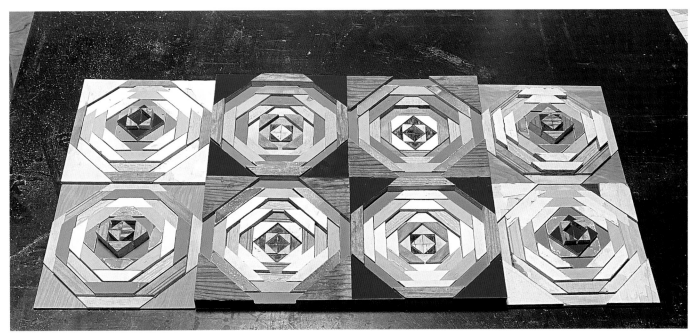

**10** **Measure the collection.** Lay all your completed blocks out in their final placement. I chose to flip-flop the rows for maximum contrast. Measure the width and the length of this final layout.

**11** **Cut the backing board and glue down.** Cut the full backing board to exactly the measurement you took in step 10, or to ¹⁄₁₆" (0.2cm) shorter widthwise and lengthwise. The edges will not be visible because it will be recessed into the tabletop frame. This allows you to skip the usual backing board trimming step. Glue down all eight blocks to the backing board secure against the 90° corner frame. Use some long clamps and scrap pieces of lumber to secure it flat to the table while the glue dries. You've finished the assembly of the design itself. Now it's time to make the coffee table!

# Making the Coffee Table

*Many of the tools required for this coffee table build are also required for the quilt design build and are not repeated here; listed here are only the additional items needed for the coffee table build.

## TOOLS

- ❏ Framing nailer
- ❏ Cordless drill
- ❏ Impact driver
- ❏ 1" (2.5cm) paddle bit
- ❏ ¹⁄₁₆" (0.2cm) drill bit
- ❏ Countersink bit
- ❏ Belt sander
- ❏ Putty knife
- ❏ Mallet
- ❏ File

## MATERIALS

- ❏ Wood filler
- ❏ White spray paint
- ❏ Satin clear spray
- ❏ Nails, 16-gauge 1¼" (3.2cm) finishing nails
- ❏ 10-gauge 3" (7.6cm) deck screws

## CUTTING LIST

*This cutting list differs from all other cutting lists in the book in that it lists the raw purchased lumber and materials that are cut down during the instructions for the build, not the final cut shapes and dimensions.

| QUANTITY | SIZE & SHAPE | MATERIAL |
|---|---|---|
| 4 | Strip: 3½" x 8', 1½" thick (8.9 x 243.8cm, 3.8cm thick) | 2x4 prime whitewood stud (for horizontal framing) |
| 2 | Strip: 3½" x 8', 3½" thick (8.9 x 243.8cm, 8.9cm thick) | 4x4 Douglas fir (for vertical framing) |
| 1 | Strip: 1½" x 8', ¾" thick (3.8 x 243.8cm, 1.9cm thick) | 1x2 pine (for quilt design ledge) |
| 1 | Dowel: 48" long, 1" diameter (122cm long, 2.5cm diameter) | Round wooden dowel (for pegs) |
| 2 | Rectangle: 3' x 6', ³⁄₁₆" thick (92 x 183cm, 0.5cm thick) | Clear acrylic sheet (for protective tabletops) |

Here is a preview of the basic table frame that you will build, before the dowels, quilt design, and acrylic tabletop are added. Use it as a visual guide as you work.

## Make the Horizontal Frames

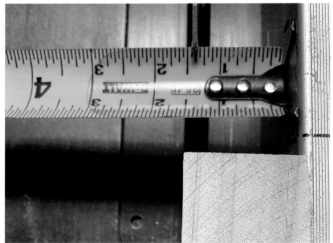

1 **Rip down your 2x4s.** Start by sanding all your 2x4s and 4x4s with 120-grit sandpaper on a palm sander. Make sure you have a general-purpose blade or ripping blade on the table saw. Then rip your 2x4s down to make them 1⅜" x 3" (3.5 x 7.6cm). They look nicer when they are a little smaller rather than the basic 2x4 size. It also looks nicer to have a sharper edge around the inside of the frames rather than the well-rounded edge of a 2x4 fresh from the lumberyard. Sand those freshly cut surfaces again to knock down the sharpness of the new edges just a little.

2 **Cut the pieces for the horizontal frames.** Each of the two horizontal frames is made from your cut-down 2x4s and has mitered corners, like other mitered frames from other projects in the book. (Refer to steps 21–22 from the Prosperity Block Shadowbox project for more guidance if needed.) The inside dimension of each frame should be just a hair larger than the measurement of your built quilt design. For example, my final block assembly is 23¼" (59.1cm) wide, so I made sure my cuts from inside angle to inside angle were 23⅜" (59.4cm). This allows just enough space for the art to slide into its frame without being forced. Once you have the piece cut at the length you want it, you can trace the remaining cuts straight from that piece.

**3** **Glue and nail.** After you have cut eight pieces (four for each of the two horizontal frames), glue and nail the corners with a framing nailer. Clamp your frames to the table when you shoot the nails to avoid any shifting. Double-check that the rectangle is true by measuring the diagonal in both directions. Clamp one side of the rectangle to the table while doing this and adjust the frame until you achieve equal measurements, then clamp all corners down and let the glue dry.

**4** **Rip and cut the ledge for the top frame.** Only the top frame requires an inner ledge on which to rest the quilt block design. Take your 1x2s, which are actually ¾" x 1½" (1.9 x 3.8cm), and rip them in half to ¾" x ¾" (1.9 x 1.9cm). The corners of the ledge can be butt-jointed—no need to miter them. Measure the inside dimension of your top frame and cut your material to line the inside.

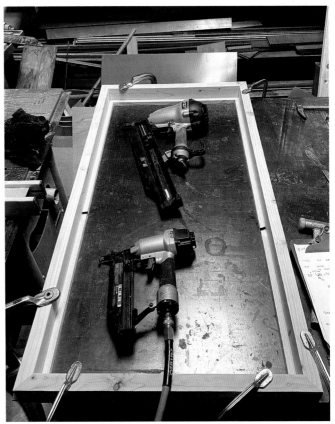

**5** **Attach the ledge.** Glue and nail the ledge with a finishing nailer with the ledge pushed flat to the table.

# Make the Vertical Leg Frames

6 **Cut the uprights of the leg frames.** The already-sanded 4x4s will be made into the vertical leg frames. These are U-shaped, and the horizontal frames sit inside them. First, cut the four uprights of the U-shaped frames. Cut a 45° angle at the end of one of the 4x4s, then measure up 18" (45.7cm) on the long side of the angle and cut a 90° angle. (This means the coffee table will be 18" [45.7cm] tall.) This completes one upright; repeat to cut a total of four uprights.

7 **Cut the crossbars of the leg frames.** The uprights you just cut will form mitered corners with the crossbars. Measure the width of your horizontal frames from outer edge to outer edge; mine measured 26" (66cm). This is how long the short side of each of your two crossbars needs to be. Cut a 45° angle on one end of a 4x4, then measure and mark your short side length and cut another 45° angle. Repeat to create the second crossbar.

8 **Assemble the vertical leg frames.** Glue and shoot two framing nails up through the bottom of the crossbars into each upright, or, if you don't have a framing nailer available to use, drill two ⅟₁₆" (0.2cm) pilot holes for each vertical leg up through the bottom 4x4 crossbars and then countersink. Then, screw 3" (7.6cm) 10-gauge deck screws up into the verticals. Check the 90° angle of each vertical and measure from corner to corner to check if they are true. Once everything checks out, clamp it all down and place a brace between the uprights to prevent them from drifting while the glue dries. When the frames are dry, sand the joints.

# Assemble the Frames Together

**9 Measure and arrange the frame piece.** We will place the vertical legs spaced out so that the middle set of four blocks of your quilt assembly fits between the legs. Clamp the U-shaped vertical leg frames to the worktable with the uprights pointing up. Place the bottom horizontal rectangle frame (the ledgeless frame) all the way down into the horseshoe until it is resting on the crossbars. Measure from the inside left short edge of the horizontal frame to 12" (30.5cm), and make sure the inner side of your left leg is flush with that measurement. (If the individual blocks in your assembly are slightly different than the assumed 12" [30.5cm] measurement, use your block size to determine the placement of the leg instead.) Do this at the other end of the frame too. Double-check that the bottom shelf is level and that the uprights are pointing vertically at true 90° angles.

**10 Screw the bottom together.** Countersink and screw two 10-gauge deck screws at each of the four intersection points to join the horizontal frame to the vertical leg frames. Fill these holes and any other nail holes or blemishes with wood filler.

**11 Measure and check the top.** Measure the width of your acrylic sheet—it should be ³⁄₁₆" (0.5cm)— and mark that measurement down from the top of each upright. This is where you will later attach the tabletop frame—with the top flush with the mark—in order to make the acrylic surface flush with the top of the 4x4 legs, as shown here.

**12** **Attach the top.** Clamp, glue, and screw the tabletop into place, ledge down, using a clamp underneath the tabletop to hold it at its proper height.

**13** **Check your progress.** Your basic frame is done! It should look like this at this point.

## Add the Wooden Pegs

**14** **Mark the top peg hole placement.** The top pegs are centered to both the horizontal 1x3 frame and the vertical 4x4 legs. Use a speed square to mark a line on the front (outer) face of the 4x4 leg flush with where the bottom of the 3" (7.6cm) board is. Then place a combination or speed square at that mark to find the horizontal center of the 4x4—1¾" (4.4cm). Then measure 1½" (3.8cm) up from there to mark the center of the 3" (7.6cm) board. This gives you the final peg hole placement for the top pegs. (The photo shows it ready to be drilled, which happens later.)

**15** **Mark the middle and bottom peg hole placement.** Place a square on the table, measure up 1¾" (4.4cm) and mark, and measure up 5" (12.7cm) and mark. Then, hash these marks at 1¾" (4.4cm) across (half the width of the 4x4 legs). This gives you the final peg hole placement for the middle and bottom pegs; the bottom pegs are centered to the crossbar 4x4s, and the middle pegs are simply placed 5" (12.7cm) up from the bottom, not centered on the bottom horizontal frame like the top pegs are.

**16** **Drill the top peg holes.** Only the top pegs are functional. These holes need to be at least 4¼" (10.8cm) deep so that they pierce the horizontal frame wood. It adds extra support to have the peg go all the way into the horizontal frame. Put tape around the stem of a 1" (2.5cm) paddle bit at the 4⅜" (11.1cm) mark to help you know how deep you are, then drill with your impact driver. Drill all four top peg holes.

**17** **Drill the middle and bottom peg holes.** The remaining pegs are just aesthetic. Their holes don't need to be as deep—1" (2.5cm) to 2" (5.1cm) is fine. Drill these holes with the same paddle bit. In this photo, you can see I've started to cut (but not yet sanded) the pegs, which is the next step.

**18** **Cut and sand the pegs.** Cut the 1" (2.5cm)–diameter dowel into twelve pegs. Each peg will be inserted into a hole with ¾" (1.9cm) sticking out. You need four pegs that are 5" (12.7cm) long for the top holes. Cut the remaining eight pegs to be just 2"–3" (5.1–7.6cm) long, depending on the depth of your holes. After you cut the pegs, round the to-be-exposed edges with a medium-grit belt sander or spin them on a file.

Pineapple Ice Queen Coffee Table **127**

**19** **Insert the pegs.** Apply some wood glue on the ends of each peg, with a little bit along the sides by the end, and tap each peg in using a mallet. Clean off any glue that oozes out of the hole with a damp rag. Remember to leave ¾" (1.9cm) of the peg sticking out from the legs. Let the glue dry.

**20** **Fill and sand.** Apply wood filler to all the nail and screw holes. You also might need some in the corner joints or other gaps that may need to be filled. Let it dry, and then sand away the filler and glue from around the pegs and joints with 120-grit sandpaper on your palm sander. Make one last pass with fine-grit sandpaper to get the surfaces super smooth. Also, round off all the corners of the frames and the top edges of the 4x4 legs—you don't want any harsh edges that might make human contact.

## Apply a Faux Aged Finish

**21** **Spray a coat of paint.** Here is a quick and easy way to achieve a white pickled look or, as some might call it, a "shabby chic" effect. First, connect the air hose of your air compressor with the blower attachment and blow all the dust off the table. Then grab a cheap can of white spray paint. Do a quick, consistent, light coat of paint all over the table, holding the can about 10" (25.4cm) away. Make smooth, sweeping motions with your arm. Let the paint fully dry.

**22** **Sand the paint.** Sand the whole table using a palm sander and 220-grit sandpaper. The sanding brings back out some of the wood's natural tone. Sand lightly or heavily, depending on the final look you're going for—the more you sand, the more paint will come off, and the more distressed the finish will seem.

**23** **Apply the finish.** When you are happy with the look, blow off the dust again and give it a quick wipe-down with a lint-free towel. Then spray two light coats of clear satin spray over the entire piece, holding the can about 8" (20.3cm) away and allowing the first coat to dry for a minute before proceeding to the second coat. After the second coat, lightly sand by hand with 400-grit sandpaper. This knocks off any little burs or small debris that might have dried in the clear coat. Blow it off one more time with your air hose and add one final coat of clear spray. Let it dry for at least an hour.

## Cut the Acrylic Tabletop

**24** **Measure and cut the sheets.** You will need to cut down the two standard-sized pieces of acrylic sheet to size to fit your horizontal frames. Measure your frames (outer edge to outer edge) to determine your exact measurements. Subtract ¹⁄₁₆" (0.2cm) or ⅛" (0.3cm) from your dimensions, depending on how rounded your top edges are on the frames. You can have the pieces cut for you if you purchase the sheets at the store, or, if you plan on cutting them yourself, follow these instructions. My final dimensions to cut to were 25⅞" x 49⅜" (65.7 x 125.4cm). Put a finishing blade on your table saw. Set the fence to 25⅞" (65.7cm) and rip. Be a little more patient cutting the acrylic than you are with wood. Since most table saws' ruler sides don't extend past 36" (91.4cm) or 48" (122cm), you need to mark the length dimension, 49⅜" (125.4cm), on the sheet. Set the blade on the remnant side and rip.

**25** **Check the fit and file.** Check the size of the newly cut material. Make sure there isn't overhang and that it rests neatly in its frame how you want it. If you are satisfied, file all the edges. Round off the top edges of the sheet a bit more than the bottom edges, and round the four corners as well. Put the acrylic back on, and you're done!

# Patterns

All of the patterns here are presented at full size to be easily photocopied. For a printable PDF of the patterns, please contact Fox Chapel Publishing at customerservice@foxchapelpublishing.com, stating the ISBN and title of the book in the subject line.

## Lattice Square Wall Hanging Pattern

### Grid: 1½" (3.8cm)

Photocopy at 100%. Make nine copies and assemble per layout diagram on page 39.

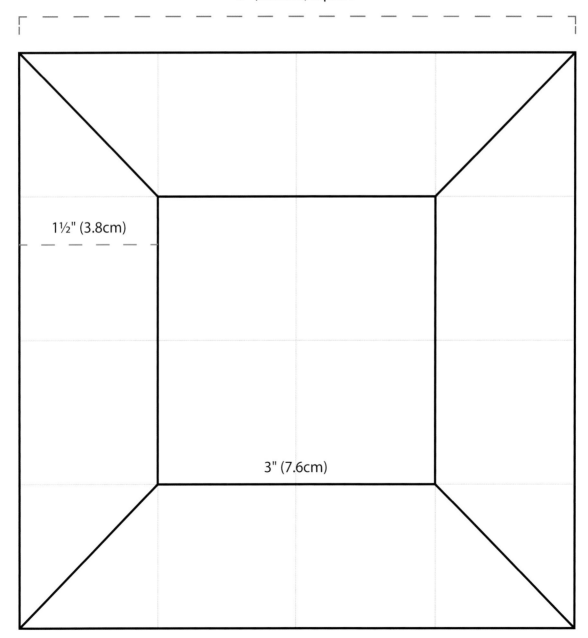

6" (15.2cm) square

1½" (3.8cm)

3" (7.6cm)

# Goose Tracks Woodburned Wall Art Pattern

Grid: 1½" (3.8cm)

Photocopy at 100%. Make four copies and assemble per layout diagram on page 61.

7½" (19.1cm) square

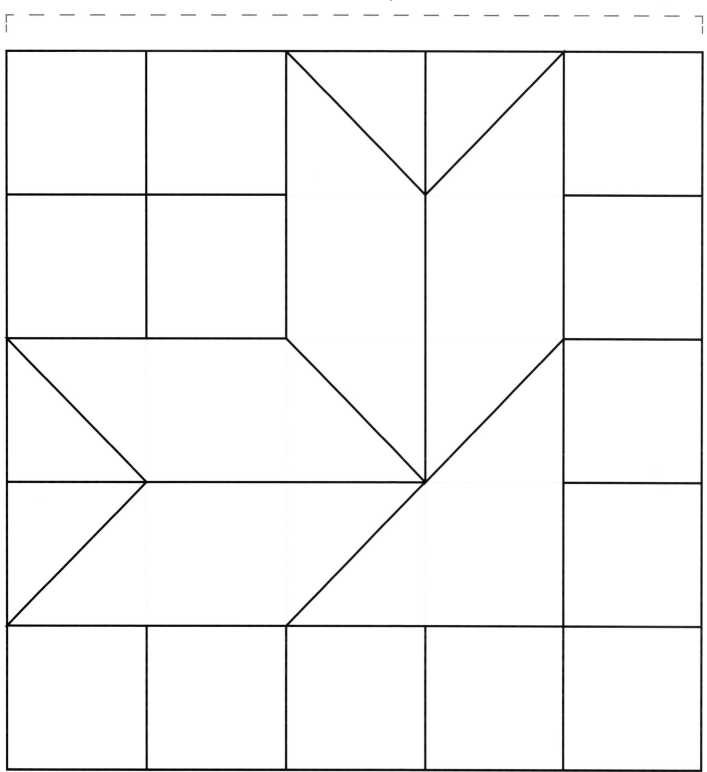

# Prosperity Block Shadowbox Pattern

### Grid: 1" (2.5cm)

Photocopy at 100%.
Make four copies of each half.
With one piece of each side,
align and tape the halves
together at the dotted line as
seen in the assembled pattern
diagram. Repeat for a total of
four blocks and combine to
create the final piece seen in
the full layout diagram on
page 49.

9" (22.9cm) square

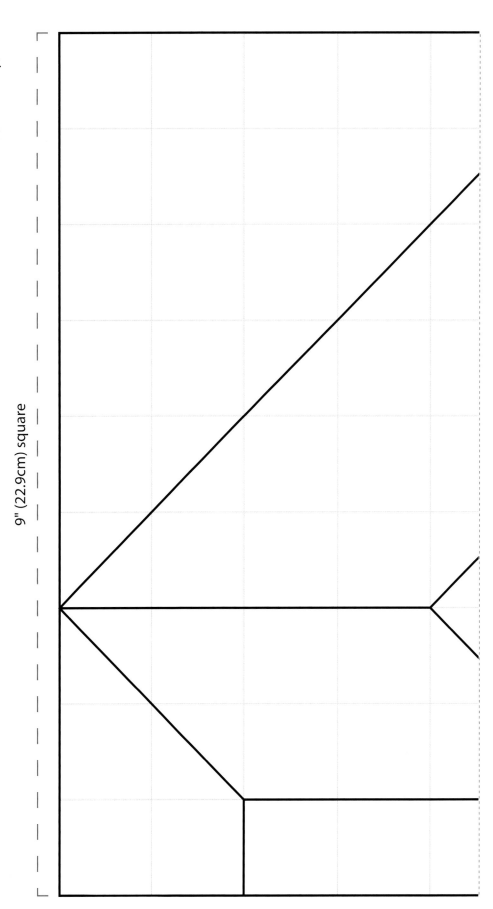

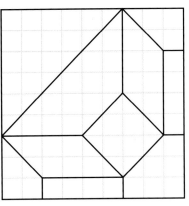

Assembled pattern

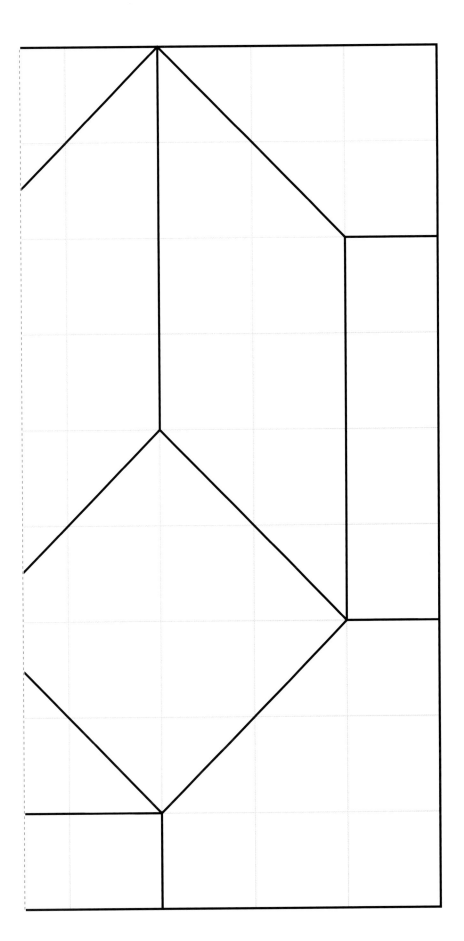

# Radiant Lone Star Wood Tapestry Pattern

Grid: 1" (2.5cm)

Photocopy at 100%. Make two copies of each half, combine the halves into single pieces by taping along the dotted lines, and assemble per layout diagram on page 81.

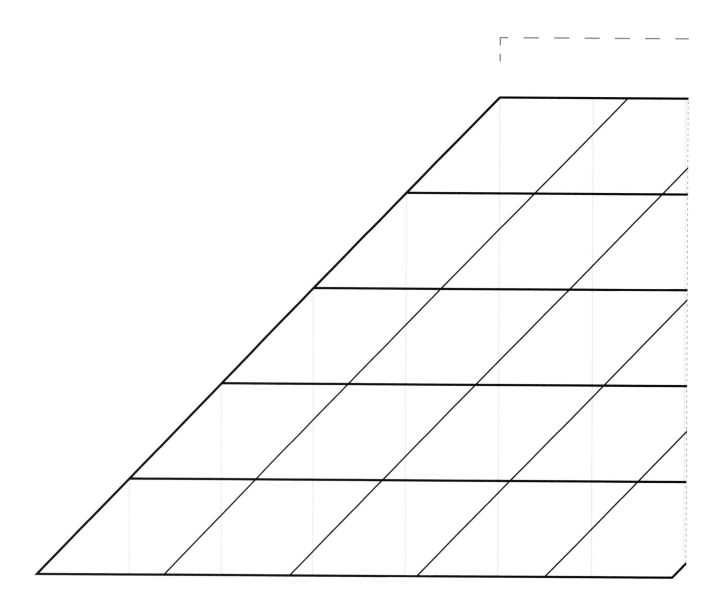

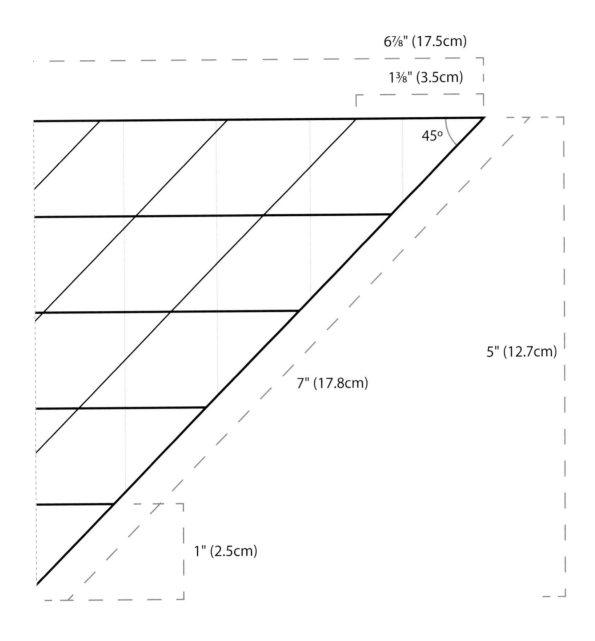

6⅞" (17.5cm)

1⅜" (3.5cm)

45°

5" (12.7cm)

7" (17.8cm)

1" (2.5cm)

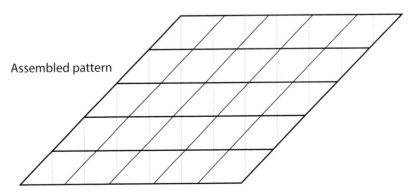

Assembled pattern

# Log Cabin Wall Quilt Pattern

### Grid: 1" (2.5cm)

Photocopy at 100%.
Make one copy of each half
and combine them into a
single piece by taping along
the dotted lines per layout
diagram on page 93.

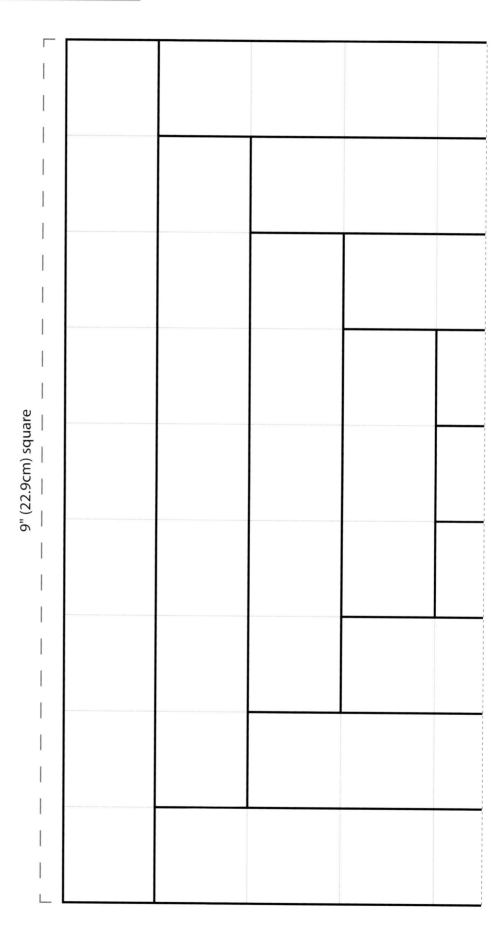

9" (22.9cm) square

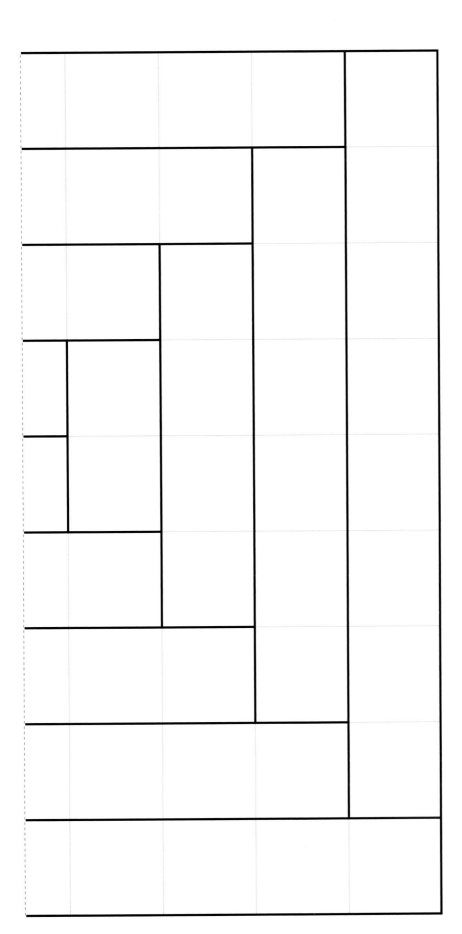

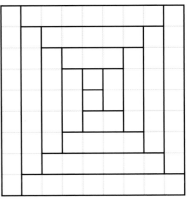

Assembled pattern

# Festival of Stars Door Pattern

Grid: 1" (2.5cm)

Photocopy at 100%. Make one copy each of the star and the pinwheel and combine per project photo on page 103.

8" (20.3cm) square

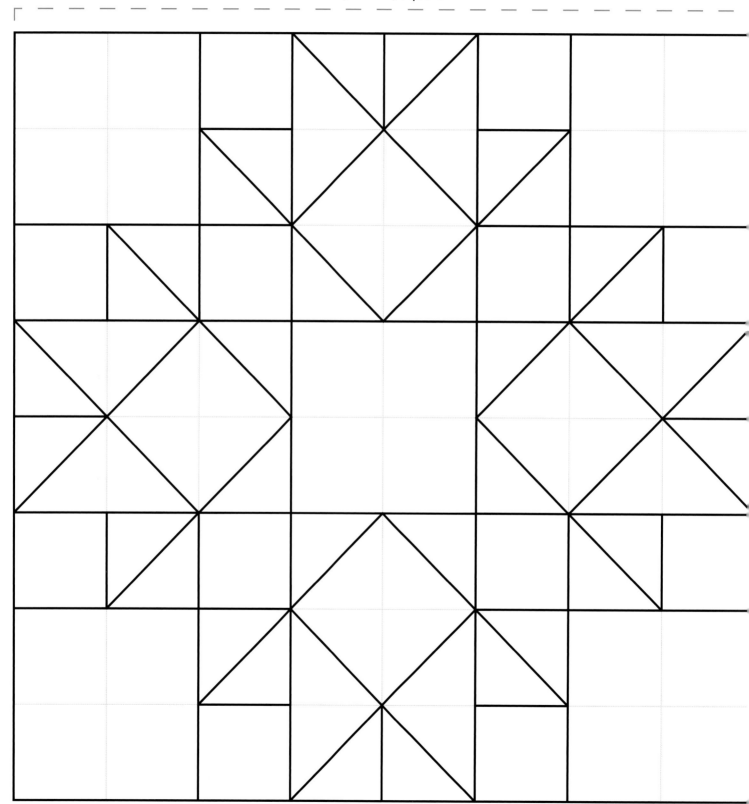

6" (15.2cm) square

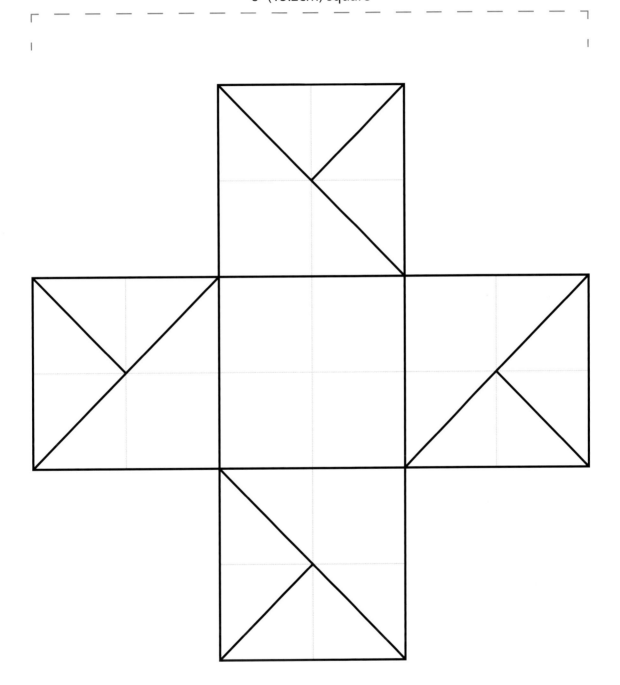

# Star and Wreath Desk Décor Pattern

**Grid: 1" (2.5cm)**

Photocopy at 100%. Make four copies and assemble per layout diagram on page 71.

7" (17.8cm) square

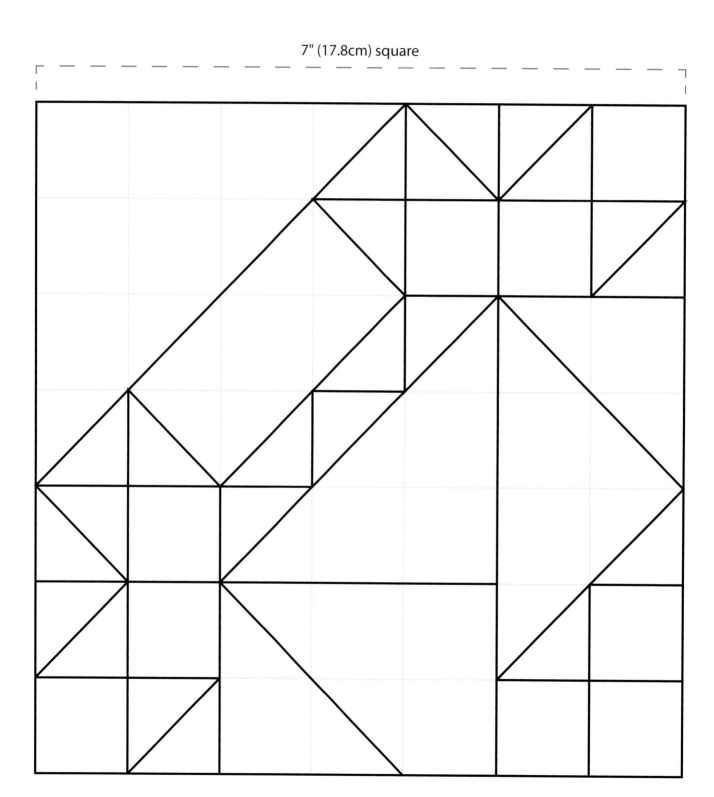

# Pineapple Ice Queen Coffee Table Pattern

## Grid: 1" (2.5cm)

Photocopy at 100%. Make four copies and assemble per layout diagram on page 117.

6" (15.2cm) square

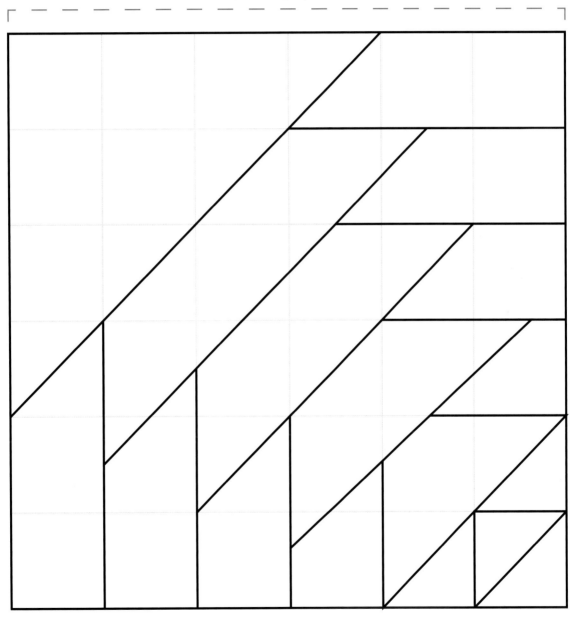

# About the Artist

Houston-born artist Troy Murrah moved to Los Angeles more than 20 years ago, after earning a BFA in Studio Art from the University of Texas, Austin. He worked in production design while doing his visual art on the side. Concurrently, he toured internationally with his two-piece band, Restavrant. During all of this, he continued to do carpentry-type work—production and set design, designing and building recording studios, and, now, producing a line of home accents and wall hangings. Through all of these jobs, he picked up a habit of saving interesting leftover material (wood, metal, doors, shelves, etc.) that he couldn't bear to see go to waste, even though he did not know, at the time, what he was saving it for.

In December 2017, his mother, Judy Murrah, passed away. She was an avid quilter, art educator, author, and textile designer. As a process of feeling close to her and his childhood, he revisited his visual art with a new body of work—she always wanted him to do something "quilt-inspired" with his art.

This inspiration has turned into a great way to use up salvaged material and bring new life to the old. Starting with a solo art show in November 2018 at 4th Street Vine in Long Beach, California, Troy presented pieces that were personal commentaries on the strength of our mothers, the ability to turn even the humblest living conditions into a home, and remembering that chivalry is not dead. Since then, he has received an overwhelmingly positive response, including invitations to speak at guild meetings, commissions, and press.

Taking on a life of its own, Troy's body of work continues to expand with new artistic additions created on an ongoing basis. Overall, his artwork pays homage to tradition and remains very sentimental, drawing on themes related to normal everyday life at home, or even to some of his bizarre "storybook"-like experiences, while offering a fresh take on the traditional quilt. The wall hangings he makes range in size from 8" x 8"

(20.3 x 20.3cm) to 7' x 6' (213 x 183cm), and he has also expanded to making functional furniture pieces.

Along with his wife, Michelle, he runs Built Quilt, a brand of quilt-inspired home accents, celebrating timeless quilt patterns beyond the cloth. The pair resides in Torrance, California, with their two young sons, Thompson and Tyrus. Their video series, "Wood Riddance," can be found online and streaming. To learn more about Troy and his work, visit *www.BuiltQuilt.com*, or find him on Facebook and Instagram @BuiltQuilt.

## Acknowledgments

Without my mom, Judy Murrah, I wouldn't be doing what I am doing. She gave me life, inspiration, and the encouragement to follow through as an artist. Thank you, Mom, for urging me to use quilt designs as an element in my art.

And, many thanks:

To my whole family—my dad, Tom, my brother, Todd, and my sister, Holly, for influencing me, each in their own creative way, and being my "home" while growing up.

To my wife's family for being supportive, especially my mother-in-law, Farida, for helping me obtain more time in the studio and giving me an excuse to have a "beverage break" at Ahma and YaYa's to recharge.

To the Fox Chapel team—Amelia for reaching out to me and getting the ball rolling, and Colleen for all her amazing work while "swimming in shapes."

And most importantly:

To my caring wife, Michelle "Meesh"—she is the beautiful magic sorceress behind the curtain. None of this would be happening without her nonstop intellectual wit, pep-talking, time managing, business making, creative brainstorming, and above-average sense of humor. And to our sons, Thompson and Tyrus, for being patient with Daddy while he makes art.

# Index

Note: Page numbers in *italics* indicate projects and patterns (in parentheses).
Page numbers in **bold** indicate gallery items.

## A

aging screws, 33
assembling, gluing and, 30
automotive body filler, 31

## B

*A Big Sting Comeback*, **11**
brad nailer, 26
Broken Star (or Dutch Rose) quilt block, **8–9**
Burgoyne Surrounded quilt block, **12**

## C

caulking, as filler, 31
chop saw, 22–23
circular saw, 22–23
clamps, 25
coffee table, *114–29, (141)*
cordless drill/impact driver, 26
cutting specific shapes, 28–29

## D

Diamond Log Cabin Star quilt block, **11**
distressed looks, 31–32
*Doe, a Deer*, **14**
door, festival of stars, *100–113, (138–39)*
Double Irish Chain quilt block, **16**
drill, cordless, 26

## F

*Farida's Enchanted Wallpaper*, **12**
fasteners, 25
Festival of Stars Door, *100–113, (138–39)*
files, 24
fillers and filling, 31
finishing nailer, 26
framing nailer, 26

## G

gallery, **8–17**
   about: beauty of reclaimed materials, 17
   *A Big Sting Comeback*, **11**
   *Doe, a Deer*, **14**
   *Farida's Enchanted Wallpaper*, **12**
   *Go West, Mary*, **8–9**
   *Heads Are Important Helmet Hanger*, **15**
   *'70s Ski Party*, **10**
   *The Strength of a Scorpion Mother*, **13**
   *You Make Me Feel*, **16**
glossary of terms, 20
gluing and assembling, 30

*Go West, Mary*, **8–9**
Goose Tracks Woodburned Wall Art, *58–67, (131)*
grinder, 23

## H

hailers, 26
hammer, 25
hanging techniques, 33
*Heads Are Important Helmet Hanger*, **15**

## I

impact driver, 26

## L

latex caulking, 31
Lattice Square Wall Hanging, *36–45, (130)*
levels, 25
Log Cabin quilt block, **13**
Log Cabin Wall Quilt, *90–99, (136–37)*
Lone Star quilt block, **15**
Luan, about, 20
lumber sizes, 21

## M

materials, 20–21
   glossary of terms, 20
   purchased, 21
   reclaimed and recycled, 20–21
   tools and, 22–26
MDF (medium-density fiberboard), about, 20
miter (chop) saw, 22–23
mitering, 30
mosaics
   about: this book and, 6
   getting started, 19
   making (*See* projects; techniques, tips, and tricks)
   materials for, 20–21
   tools for making, 22–26
Mother's Choice quilt block, **10**

## N

nails and screws, 25

## O

OSB (oriented strand board), about, 20

## P

painting, distressing, staining, 31–32
palm sander, 24
paper, for patterns, 22

parallelograms, cutting, 29
particle board, about, 20
patterns, *130–41. See also* quilt blocks
    about: paper for, 22; using, 27
    Festival of Stars Door, *(138–39)*
    Goose Tracks Woodburned Wall Art, *(131)*
    Lattice Square Wall Hanging, *(130)*
    Log Cabin Wall Quilt, *(136–37)*
    Pineapple Ice Queen Coffee Table, *(141)*
    Prosperity Block Shadowbox, *(132–33)*
    Radiant Lone Star Wood Tapestry, *(134–35)*
    Star and Wreath Desk Décor, *(140)*
Pineapple Ice Queen Coffee Table, *114–29, (141)*
Plexiglas®, about, 20
plywood, about, 20
projects
    about: overview of, 35; techniques for making (*See* techniques, tips, and tricks)
    Festival of Stars Door, *100–113, (138–39)*
    Goose Tracks Woodburned Wall Art, *58–67, (131)*
    Lattice Square Wall Hanging, *36–45, (130)*
    Log Cabin Wall Quilt, *90–99, (136–37)*
    Pineapple Ice Queen Coffee Table, *114–29, (141)*
    Prosperity Block Shadowbox, *46–57, (132–33)*
    Radiant Lone Star Wood Tapestry, *78–89, (134–35)*
    Star and Wreath Desk Décor, *68–77, (140)*
Prosperity Block Shadowbox, *46–57, (132–33)*
purchased materials, 21

**Q**
quadrilaterals, cutting, 28–29
quilt blocks
    Broken Star (or Dutch Rose), **8–9**
    Burgoyne Surrounded, **12**
    Diamond Log Cabin Star, **11**
    Double Irish Chain, **16**
    Log Cabin, **13** (*See also* Log Cabin Wall Quilt)
    Lone Star, **15**
    Mother's Choice, **10**
    Radiant (Lone) Star, **14** (*See also* Radiant Lone Star Wood Tapestry)

**R**
Radiant (Lone) Star quilt block, **14**
Radiant Lone Star Wood Tapestry, *78–89, (134–35)*
reclaimed and recycled materials, 17, 20–21
rectangles, cutting, 28
router, 26

**S**
sander, palm, 24
sandpaper, 24
saws, types of, 22–23
screws, aging, 33
*'70s Ski Party*, **10**
shadowbox, *46–57, (132–33)*
shapes, cutting, 28–29
squares (tools), 24
squares, cutting, 28
staining, painting, distressing, 31–32
Star and Wreath Desk Décor, *68–77, (140)*
stenciling and woodburning, 32–33
*The Strength of a Scorpion Mother*, **13**

**T**
table, work/layout, 22
table saw, 22
tape measure, 24
techniques, tips, and tricks
    aging screws, 33
    cutting specific shapes, 28–29
    filling, 31
    gluing and assembling, 30
    hanging projects, 33
    mitering, 30
    painting, distressing, staining, 31–32
    using patterns, 27
    woodburning and stenciling, 32–33
tools, 22–26
trapezoids, cutting, 29
triangles, cutting, 28

**U**
underlayment, about, 20

**W**
wall hangings/decor. *See* projects
wood
    nominal and actual lumber sizes, 21
    types of, defined, 20
wood filler, 31
woodburning and stenciling, 32–33. *See also* Goose Tracks Woodburned Wall Art
worktable/layout table, 22

**Y**
*You Make Me Feel*, **16**